WHICH WAY FOR
CATHOLIC PENTECOSTALS?

WHICH WAY
FOR CATHOLIC
PENTECOSTALS?

J. Massyngberde Ford

HARPER & ROW, PUBLISHERS

NEW YORK, HAGERSTOWN, SAN FRANCISCO, LONDON

FIRST EDITION

Library of Congress Cataloging in Publication Data

Ford, Josephine Massyngberde.
    Which way for Catholic pentecostals?

    Bibliography: p.
    1. Pentecostalism.   I. Title.
BX2350.57.F67   1976   262'.001   75-36757
ISBN 0-06-062672-0

76 77 78 79 10 9 8 7 6 5 4 3 2 1

282.4
F699

Contents

Prologue

Neo-Pentecostalism or, as some prefer to call it, the Charismatic Renewal, is an experience affecting growing numbers of persons in mainline churches. In an article in the *New Catholic World*, Ralph Martin, overall coordinator of the Word of God Community, Ann Arbor, Michigan, and editor of the *New Covenant*, estimates that the number of Roman Catholics involved in the movement at present is about three hundred fifty thousand. Forty countries were represented at the International Conference held at the University of Notre Dame,[1] Notre Dame, Indiana, in June 1974. The *Directory of Catholic Charismatic Prayer Groups* listed twenty-four hundred groups in fifty-four countries in 1974.

This book concerns Catholic Neo-Pentecostalism, a prayer movement that originated at Duquesne University, Pittsburgh, Pennsylvania, in 1967. Catholic Neo-Pentecostalism is a special kind of spirituality which may not be suitable for all but which has brought many changes to innumerable individuals. It began as informal, spontaneous prayer meetings, characterized by an acute experimental awareness of the presence of God, experienced both by the individuals comprising the group and by the group as a whole. This phenomenon is called the "release" or "baptism" in the Spirit. Catholic Neo-Pentecostalism is also distinguished by the use of such charismatic gifts as speaking in tongues (glossolalia), interpretation of tongues, prophecy, healing, inspirational interpretation of Scripture, and, occasionally, exorcism. Since 1967 it has spread throughout the world and in many places is seeking to establish more or less permanent communities of Christians. Some of these communities are Catholic, and some are ecumenical.

However, the founders of the movement, Dr. William G. Storey, Dr. Ralph Keifer, and Mrs. Roberta Keifer, have withdrawn from participation because of the movement's increasing structuredness and authoritarianism and also because of the tendency of many groups to lose their Catholic distinctives. The most powerful centers of the movement in North America are in Ann Arbor, Michigan, and South Bend, Indiana, where both the national and the international organizational offices are situated. Nowadays only a small group meets on the Notre Dame University campus, whereas formerly several hundred assembled. At present the Ann Arbor and South Bend part of the movement is highly structured, with an initiatory rite, post "Spirit release" instruction, and great emphasis on community (often covenanted community) life. A male lay hierarchy guides this part of the movement, and these groups have just purchased a nine-story hotel in South Bend.

It would seem that the "oligarchy," which has hardly changed membership since the beginning of the movement, has not had an opportunity to stand back and reflect upon the direction of the leadership and its "theology" or the movement's increasingly ecumenical characteristics. Moreover, many theologians associated with the movement have either approached it quite uncritically or have taken a purely academic stance in relation to it. The latter have written using official documents, such as material from the second Vatican Council in the 1960s and the Malines Document of 1974, written in Belgium. They have not availed themselves of oral tradition as it is found in tape recordings or the abundant popular literature that flows through the hands of members of the numerous groups. In this book, I have attempted to correlate and systematize the main tenets of the movement. My intent has not been to criticize its leaders, who are sincere, profoundly dedicated, hard-working men and women, but to serve as a guide to bishops, priests, other Catholics, and other interested persons who wish to understand this type of spirituality.

I have written with favor and appreciation of Pentecostalism in five books and various articles, and I do not wish to repeat my remarks here. I am still an active member of the Pentecostal Renewal but also venture into other charismatic areas, such as the ordination of women and the ministry concerning death and dying. Currently I teach New Testament at the University of Notre Dame, where I have been closely associated with Pentecostalism from its beginning. I use the word *Pentecostal* to denote the spirituality under discussion, for I believe that anyone who has an intimate relationship with Jesus is a charismatic. This book describes two different facets of Roman Catholic Pentecostalism that have arisen over the past seven years. I am a theologian specializing in New Testament studies and not a qualified psychologist or sociologist, but on matters discussed here I have sought the counsel of specialists in these two areas. Rather than passing judgments, this book poses questions, although it will be clear to which facet of the movement I myself incline. I still feel that Pentecostal Renewal is inspired by the Holy Spirit and has great potential for the church.

My appreciation goes to Susan Arterian for her careful editing of this book and also to the typists at Notre Dame who typed the manuscript so accurately.

This book is dedicated to two charismatic friends, Mrs. Ann

Walshe and Dr. Peter Walshe, and their family, who have been
a source of inspiration and joy to me. There is a saying, "Perhaps
we are permitted to be comfortable because we are not fit to be
heroic." Ann and Peter have chosen with deep love to comfort
the afflicted and to afflict the comfortable. This is the essence
of true religion of which only heroines and heroes are capable.

Notes

1. *Notre Dame* is a misnomer since the Pentecostals have
practically abandoned the campus except for the International
Conferences. The Men's Shepherds' Conference was hosted by the
University of Notre Dame, although it was not sponsored by her,
in the summer of 1976.

WHICH WAY FOR
CATHOLIC PENTECOSTALS?

1
The Development of Community Life

The Two Facets

From my investigations and from my experience I have distinguished two forms or types of Catholic Neo-Pentecostalism. I am aware that the word *type* is a sociological term but feel that it is legitimate to use in this case since it is possible to identify two distinct sociological "principles" in the movement today. The first type has a paraecclesial structure; a teaching, advisory, and executive magisterium; and a disciplinary system. It appears to be modeled on (a) the Church of the Redeemer, Houston, Texas; (b) the Word of God Community, Ann Arbor, Michigan, and the People of Prayer Community, South Bend, Indiana; and (c) the Bruderhof-Hutterian community model as described in Benjamin Zablocki's book *The Joyful Community*. The second type of Catholic Neo-Pentecostalism is flexible and less structured. It is fully integrated with the theology and sacramentality of the contemporary Catholic church, is open to non-Pentecostal influences, and is deeply interested in Eastern Orthodox theology. This type is similar to the early Franciscan and Dominican spirituality.

In the first part of this book, attention is given to Type I, and my remarks conclude with reflections on an apparent affinity between this type and the Radical Reformers of the sixteenth century. I discuss Type I first because its leaders hold the largest number of seats on the committees that guide the movement. On the Service Committee, the only executive body in the whole international movement, adherents to Type I hold all the seats save three. In his *Statement on Behalf of the Catholic Charismatic Renewal Service Committee*, made in May 1975, Kevin Ranaghan, president of the Charismatic Renewal Services and a coordinator of the people of Praise Community in South Bend, reported the names of the members of the Service Committee. All are men: one is a bishop, four are priests, and seven are lay males. Only one is from the Third World, none are black, and all are Catholic. Only two members can be designated as Type II. One is unknown to me. The rest seem to fall into the category of Type I.

In a series of articles that appeared in the *National Catholic Reporter* in 1975, special reporter Rick Casey remarked that the four leaders from Ann Arbor and South Bend have considerably more influence than the other men. All but one of the members are North American white-middle-class males. On the Steering Committee, which organizes the national and the international conventions (normally held at Notre Dame each June but held in Rome in 1975), the Type I men usually hold all the seats. There has been some revision of the Steering Committee during 1975 because of the negative criticisms raised during the year. A priest is now chairperson. However, changes do not appear to have been published. Rick Casey feels that Ranaghan's statement:

The Catholic charismatic renewal is a broad, diverse and considerably unorganized movement in which a variety of ideas and practices are current (Ranaghan, *Statement on Behalf of the Catholic Charismatic Renewal Service*, p. 1) may mask a more accurate picture:

which is that a few men here [Ann Arbor] and in South Bend wield extraordinary influence over what the hundreds of thousands of Catholic Pentecostals and Protestants associated with them . . . read . . . are taught and what direction they are likely to take (Casey, *National Catholic Reporter*, 12 September 1975, p. 4).

According to Casey's article in the same issue of the *National Catholic Reporter*, the Ann Arbor–South Bend groups control a $1.7 million service which supplies the movement with books, tape recordings, conferences, and the *New Covenant* magazine, which reaches some sixty thousand readers. The two communities have sixty persons on the payroll and many volunteers. South Bend has a $1.3 million mailing service. In the South Bend *Tribune* of April 25, 1976, it was stated that the Charismatic Renewal Services "expects to do $2 million in business this year distributing books, cassettes and records in the U.S. and around the world to approximately 125,000 customers." With due respect to Kevin Ranaghan, the sociologist Joseph Fichter in his book *The Catholic Cult of the Paraclete* calls the leadership a formal bureaucracy and concludes that the movement has at its disposal all the worldly resources necessary for the spread of a social movement: leadership, ideology, a program, communications media, and a favorable public image.

In view of the above facts, Type I is of great importance when one is considering the history of the movement, and it has been a powerful force within not only the Catholic church but also other denominations since a large percentage of non-Roman Catholics belong to some Type I groups. In his article in *Varieties of Campus Ministries*, Robert Johnson reports that over forty denominations were represented in the Word of God Community, Ann Arbor, in 1973. At present, there is a 45 percent non-Roman Catholic membership. At the beginning of this book it must be made clear that this discussion is not meant to convey any moral judgment either of Type I as a whole or of the individual leaders cited or quoted. Indeed, the words of Ulrich Zwingli and Franz Agricola about the Anabaptists can be adapted for Type I Pentecostals as well. Zwingli, writing about the Swiss brethren, said:

If you investigate their life and conduct, it seems . . . irreproachable, pious, unassuming, attractive, yea, above this world. Even those who are inclined to be critical will say that their lives are excellent (Herschberger, ed., *The Recovery of the Anabaptist Vision*, p. 44).

In his book of 1582 about the Anabaptists, Franz Agricola says:

Among the existing . . . sects there is none which in appearance leads a more modest or pious life than the Anabaptists. As concerns their outward public life they are irreproachable. No . . . swearing, strife, harsh language, no intemperate eating or drinking,[1] no outward personal display, is found among them, but . . . neatness . . . temperance, in such measure that one would suppose that they had the Holy Spirit of God (Herschberger, p. 45).

For a noncritical approach to Pentecostalism today, one may turn to Ralph Rath's articles in the June 6, 1975, *National Catholic Reporter*, "Charismatics 'Joyous' at Meeting"; Cardinal Suenens's *A New Pentecost?*, which seems to describe European Pentecostalism; and James W. Jones's *Filled with New Wine*.

Background of the Movement

Unstructured Beginnings

Catholic Neo-Pentecostalism began as a prayer movement with next to no organization; indeed, its first "meeting" was completely unplanned (O'Connor, *The Pentecostal Movement in the Catholic Church*, pp. 13–16). During the first years of its existence the phenomenon took the form of free, spontaneous prayer meetings, coincidentally similar in pattern to those described in 1 Corinthians 14:26–33 (Ford, *The Pentecostal Experience*; Cavnar, *Prayer Meetings*). There was practically no leadership, or if there were, it was rotated, usually but not always, among men; there was no initiation catechumenate nor were there "heads" and "subordinates"; the movement was open to all. The participants, on the whole, showed a marked love and a lively interest in the institutional church and a zeal for liturgical life. For instance, at Notre Dame University they attended daily public masses and weekday vespers. There was a wholesome integration with the environment and an interest in intellectual inquiry.[2] Many groups have remained like this.[3] For example, an interracial and ecumenical group in South Bend numbering about twenty, of which a third were non-Roman Catholics, began in June 1970. This was a changing group with no leadership save Jesus and no catechumenate although teaching was sometimes given at 8:00 P.M. before the meeting began at 9:00 P.M. Members were acutely aware of their surroundings and gave special consideration to how they spent their time, their attitude toward politics, and the wise use of money. One of the members was editor of the *Reformer*, a journal that emphasizes black and Christian news.[4]

Community Concept

Teaching within Type I communities has become increasingly esoteric. Only those baptized in the Spirit through "Life in the Spirit Seminars" may attend certain talks, and tape recording of meetings is not liberally permitted. Under these circumstances, fewer sources are available to scholars. I have been unable to enter into a full dialogue with the leaders of the major communities of Type I: the People of Praise, South Bend, and Word of God, Ann Arbor. Ann Arbor does not reply to my letters; South Bend will only communicate with me in letter form and has been reluctant to answer inquiries and share certain tapes. The following descriptions are based on material that *is* accessible to the general public.

On his cassette *Survey of the Catholic Charismatic Renewal,** Kevin Ranaghan teaches that, just as the sacrament of baptism leads one into a community, namely, the Church, in a similar way, the baptism of the Spirit "of its nature" leads one to an "experience of Christian life in a community, in a fellowship, in a deep relationship to one's brothers and sisters." Only when people join together in such a community can the fruits of the Spirit develop. Further, this "togetherness" creates the possibility for a strong common ministry.

Others see themselves in an eschatological era. The entire September 1972 issue of the *New Covenant* was devoted to the second coming of Jesus. In a talk given in July 1970, Ralph Martin declared that the Spirit, which was foretold by the prophets, is being poured out before our eyes and that we are "encountering the community of the Holy Spirit . . . the *first* breaking in of the kingdom." Like the apostles, Ralph Martin said, we must first experience a personal conversion, then join a community.

On his cassette *Christian Community,* Kerry Koller, one of the leaders of the John the Baptist Community, San Francisco, cites Revelation 21 and refers to the heavenly city "being born now." He explains that the city is a Christian community, not just a spiritual oneness but an actual, living community of people. Like Ranaghan, Koller thinks that it is no accident that the baptism of the Spirit calls people together. Indeed this calling together is God's plan to transform the world. Koller continues, "It is not God's plan just to form erratic prayer groups but a city, a people, a *church* [italics mine], a Christian community." He emphasizes that one must relate to some Spirit-filled community in order to receive all that the Spirit has to offer. However, Koller appears to find this community in the

---

* A list of the cassettes cited in this book is contained in the Bibliography.

Neo-Pentecostal prayer group rather than in the church as a whole. He recommends consulting the *Directory of Catholic Prayer Groups*, not the *Directory of Catholic Churches*, to find Spirit-filled Christianity. Koller refers to the prayer communities as the body of Christ. While not denying the social gospel, he speaks about the world trying to keep us from Christ, and he begs us to take our hearts from this world.

In *The Cult of the Catholic Paraclete* (p. 44), Joseph Fichter reports that from his 155 groups 71 percent of respondents agreed that the second coming of Christ is imminent. On his cassette *Growth and Decline of Prayer Groups* and in his book *In God's Providence*, John Randall, priest leader of a community in Rhode Island, is more specific. He believes that prayer groups will die out unless they have communion with one another. He says that the Lord will take the prayer groups that are prepared to follow the guidance of the Spirit and "begin to build them into His church." He states that people have a right to see the "whole body of Christ constituted" and that the Lord is trying to build a people. The use of the word *constituted* rather than *renewed* is interesting.

Although Randall does confess that the whole body of Christ is the universal church, he believes that the prayer group should be like the church in Lydia's house (Acts 16:40), that this group must be put together with God's body, and that it must be built into one body, one church. A prayer group that puts no limitation on God "will become the body of Christ eventually." Randall feels that the reason for the decline in prayer groups is that they have not come to terms with the question of leadership. If the Spirit is leading the prayer group, he will lead it to pattern its leadership on the pastoral Epistles. The leader has a charism and should not assume leadership unless he is called, like Aaron in Hebrews 5:14. Randall draws a parallel between the call to Pentecostal leadership and the call to religious life, to marriage, or to the priesthood. He compares the leadership to that found in the New Testament (see 1 Pet. 5:1–5), where it was the elders to whom the people were submissive. (The specific biblical references are mine; the original reference seems to be to bishops.) Randall speaks about the importance of prayer groups joining together for the purpose of common teaching and of their constituting the city on the mountain. He is dubious about "rolling stones," that is, those who have no firm commitment to a prayer community.

Structure and Process of the Community

The communities of Type I seem to be patterned on the Word of God Community, Ann Arbor, Michigan. Speaking at a conference organized in 1971 at Notre Dame by Paul DeCelles, a coordinator of the South Bend Community, Gerry Rauch, a member of the Ann Arbor Community, outlined what he believes to be God's plan, namely, that people are not meant to live alone but to find living situations that are based on relationships of love. Rauch recognizes that the universal church, the local church, small communities, and the house church all need one another, and, although in his talk he gives special attention to the house church, he states that one must not place all the emphasis on it. The house church is a family into which other members are taken, or a group of single people living together and sharing their lives in some stable commitment. In the house church there is a recognized head, an agreement on the nature and ideal of the living situation, a pattern of life, and financial arrangements.

THE HEAD

Rauch sees the role of the head as parallel to that of the Pope or the bishop,[5] and he asserts that without the head the house church does not function well. The role of the head must be clearly defined. His duties include evaluation; correction;

guarding the pattern of life (e.g., rebuking people for laziness); presiding at meetings, meals, and prayer; initiating decisions or, if the house cannot make a decision, making it for them; caring for each individual; judging disputes; teaching the whole house, especially concerning how to love.

In other words, the head has pastoral duties. He is also seen as the source of unity in the house church. According to Rauch, leadership of the house church cannot be left to chance; people with the gift[6] of leadership must be sought. House heads meet together once a week for guidance (presumably from each other, for no outside teacher is mentioned). The concept of "headship-subordination" in a household and of subordination to the elder of a community has progressed significantly. On cassettes entitled *Serving As Head in Christian Community* and *Elder in Christian Community*, Stephen Clark, one of the coordinators of the Ann Arbor Community, describes in detail the position and functions of such offices. A household is a unit in the community. The head stands as a father figure, and the members are sons and daughters of God. God has entrusted them to the care of the heads. The head is charged with maintaining order and rules so that disruptive elements are eliminated from prayer meetings. Members are removed from leadership if they refuse to accept the responsibility of exercising authority. Sometimes it falls to the lot of the head to change the way people pray, prophesy, or perform the music. Clark asserts that in those communities in which the head exercises proper authority there are peace and freedom; in those communities in which authority is improperly exercised, there are fear and other disadvantages. The head teaches members how to handle specific situations. He must behave like the wise man in the biblical books of Sirach and Wisdom and learn to exert the appropriate degree of pressure on people.

Clark avers that every Christian has authority, that is, an admonishing-directive role in another person's life, but the head has a more developed authority. Members must be subordinate and often obedient to him; subordination is both passive and active. The head can make all the decisions, but this does not necessarily preclude a corporate decision. Frequently it is necessary to correct someone in the Lord. The more direct and straightforward this is, the better; the head should not use indirect communication. Rebuking is one type of correction, encouragement is another, and admonishing is a third.

In a society that has lost its values, the Pentecostal heads claim to discern what is right and what is wrong; in the community there must be objective agreement about this. This sense of right and wrong must be founded on the Lord's teaching, and the head must acquire the wisdom spoken of in Wisdom and Sirach, which Clark deems written for heads to teach others. The head must have confidence that he is right and must apply correction in a warm, loving way. In the world there is a need for social approval, which is part of modern culture, but the head must remain free from this. The Lord wants to deliver all of us from the need for social approval. Some think that this kind of correction should be made in private, but Clark states that this surrounds the reproof with shame and that the correction must be in the *open and corporate*.

The head also is responsible for directing the lives of others although he does not always demand absolute obedience. For example, he must be consulted about marriage, although a personal decision is allowed. Marriage may not be contracted outside the community. The head can threaten expulsion if he is not obeyed. The head also gives authoritative teaching. Clark claims that if the head does not exercise authority, he loses it or weakness grows up in the community, but when authority is exercised properly, people begin to relate to it. Clark argues that submission does not always diminish personal initiative and individualism; this depends on the way in which headship is implemented. According to Stephen Clark, the head should draw out responsibility in people, should tell them what they need to do and that they should praise the Lord (Cassette 1127).[7]

When speaking about the elders in the Christian communities (by which Clark means the Pentecostal communities), he refers to the early church, to Acts 20 and 1 Peter 5, and shows that the elder is a shepherd, pastor, overseer, or bishop. To be subject to an elder is an act of humility. The work of an elder is fundamental to the work of an apostle; one must begin as an elder to become an apostle. Clark alludes to Ezekiel 34, the mention of the shepherd over the whole flock, and he inquires who these shepherds of Israel were. They were not priests or prophets but kings; thus the elder has a governmental function. Clark also cites 1 Thessalonians 5:12–14, which refers to those who exercise authority over the people to see that they work hard and to admonish them. Finally he speaks of Hebrews 13:17 and claims that one must obey and submit to leaders who watch over the community. They are rulers, a hegemony, and they have a real sense of authority over personal lives. The elder is more than a head of a household; he is head of a community.

Clark emphasizes again that an elder does not just oversee activities in a group, but people's very lives. Referring to Numbers 11, Clark maintains that one can only have eldership in a committed community. Eldership is instituted by the Lord and is primarily a relationship, not a function. It is analogous to a father's role. Clark finds that bishops and elders are interchangeable in 1 Timothy 3; they are a body of older men in the community. He maintains that the Lord wants us to recover the natural structure of human groups, that is, headship and subordination, and that the natural leader is the male. In the New Testament the elders are male (however, see Tit. 2:3), and male and female work better when all elders are men. The elders are a body of men, and they are worthy of respect (Cassette 1126). In light of the above, as Fichter observes (*The Catholic Cult of the Paraclete*, p. 35), it is odd how unwilling Pentecostals are to admit that the movement is organized and authoritarian. They aver "there can be no authority structure within it. The only authority can be the authority that comes from services well performed" (p. 35).* But it does seem that such a structure exists.

SUBORDINATION

Rauch sees subordination as the necessary counterpart to leadership. Although he recognizes the modern reaction to this, he asserts unequivocally that one blocks God's plan if he or she does not accept it. With regard to men and women, Rauch states quite clearly that a woman can lead only a community of women. Mrs. Paul DeCelles, who gave the talk following Rauch's at the 1971 conference, is even more emphatic upon this point. She asserts that no other arrangement works and bases her statements on what would appear to be a literal interpretation of Genesis 3.

Type I Pentecostalism seems to have adopted uncritically the teaching on headship and subordination as described in Larry Christenson's book *The Christian Family*. Christenson, a Lutheran minister, teaches the following chain of authority and responsibility: Christ, the husband, wife, and children. He omits slavery, which is accepted without any scruple in the New Testament house codes (Eph. 5:22–6:9; Col. 3:18–4:1; 1 Tim. 2:8–15, 6:1–2)—a strange omission if he wishes to be absolutely dependent on St. Paul. Christenson sees submission of the wife as a protection and as a means of spiritual power (pp. 32–54). He teaches complete, unquestioning obedience of children and advocates corporal punishment; the rod, he says, is the first response, not the last resort (pp. 55–125, 103).

* Throughout this book, page numbers when given alone refer to the last work cited.

Christenson speaks about the priesthood of parents (pp. 157–97) and even suggests open family confession (pp. 180–81).

This teaching of subordination, adopted by the covenant groups, has been a great impediment to women in the Pentecostal movement and has led to the withdrawal or exclusion of many. In his article in the *New Catholic World* of November/December 1974, Joseph Fichter remarks that two-thirds of the movement members are women but they are not given positions of leadership:

At the top level of decision-making in the national organization it is the male voice that speaks with authority. The management and editing of the movement periodical, *New Covenant*, are exclusively in male hands . . . the ideology of the movement runs counter to the general American trend toward the greater emancipation of women.

Fichter observes that this teaching is questioned by Pentecostal feminists in some of the less-organized prayer groups.

AGREEMENT ON THE IDEAL OF THE HOUSEHOLD

Rauch takes the cursillo (a Catholic "mini-retreat") principle that "only that which is binding convinces." He avers that the best way individuals can relate to one another is through a covenant agreement, that is, through an open and definite contract on *how* to relate. Such an agreement should be made before the community is formed, otherwise people come to the house church with different expectations, conflict arises, and growth is impeded.

Rauch explains how the covenant is made. Members of a group must make specific agreements, for example, to pray at 7:00 A.M. and at 10:00 P.M. Each individual must assent, and the role of the head is to be sensitive to the ways in which people react with regard to this regimentation. It is difficult to imagine how each individual can assent if some members of the community are children. The agreement must be written down; the role of the head is to remember it and to remind people of it. There must be a calling to account for "violation" (Rauch agrees that this is a strong word), and this duty is primarily that of the head although all are involved. The calling to account should not be evaluative. One must review the agreements, and this can be done at the weekly household meetings.

PATTERN OF LIFE

The pattern of life in a community would comprise a regular prayer period once or twice a day; a regular sharing; meals together (although there may be one or two nights when members do not dine together); and a house meeting. Rauch cites the example of the Ann Arbor Community, which meets at 11:30 P.M. each night "to get off one's chest all the hassles and problems" of the day. He states that before this practice began people did not know whether to share or not. Now, however, they do share, disclosures are made, and healing occurs.

Rauch admits that some married couples have experienced difficulties with the house church and that a great deal of reevaluation has been necessary. Some women cannot accept the subordinate role and complain that they entered into the covenant agreement as equals. Rauch advises them to rework the situation with reference to the male and female relationships, although he does not state how this is to be done.

After Rauch's talk, Mrs. Paul DeCelles (Cassette 121) spoke about her house church. The DeCelles have five children ranging from about seven to seventeen years of age. After a great deal of prayer they accepted two young ladies into their home. Mrs. DeCelles's evaluation was honest. She did not hide the obvious problems, such as adjustment for the children, and there can be no doubt that there is nothing lacking in Dr. and Mrs. DeCelles's zeal to commit themselves to Christ. The two young ladies bore testimony to their changed lives and the joy and freedom they experienced. One would have welcomed, however, a testimony from one of the teen-age children and also from the parents or relatives of the young ladies involved.

It is doubtful whether many twentieth-century married

women, not to mention single women who hold positions of responsibility, could accept the complete submission of women proposed by Mrs. DeCelles. It would be interesting for such households as the DeCelles's to inquire into the experience of other fully committed Christian communities, such as the Amish or the Hutterites, with regard to the adjustment required of children. Do children find it difficult to make a sufficient accommodation when faced with complete autonomy in a less-structured environment, as in a university situation?

THE SMALL COMMUNITY

The small community follows the pattern of the house church, especially with regard to headship, but it is bigger and is often divided into subcommunities. One may take as an example the community of the Word of God at Ann Arbor, Michigan. In January 1969, because the Thursday night prayer meeting had become too large and because people wished to live a more committed life, the leaders began a closed meeting for the Core Community on Monday nights. In the autumn of 1970 they divided the community into subcommunities. Four were established, and each met on Monday. According to a mimeographed report circulated by the community in 1971, the meetings follow a pattern similar to the Thursday night meetings "except that there is only one prepared talk, and it is usually given by one of the coordinators of the sub-community." Once a month there is a general meeting of the subcommunities for reception of new members who wish to make commitments, or for the "installation"[8] of leaders or for council. There are weekly celebrations of the Eucharist in three of the four sub-communities and a monthly Eucharist for the fourth sub-community although these are not official functions. This is probably because the membership of the Ann Arbor Community includes a steadily rising percentage of non-Roman Catholics although Catholics are still in the majority.

As yet I have been unable to find substantial material on the

Pentecostal lay leaders' concept of either the local church or the Roman Catholic Church. However, the November 1972 and September 1973 issues of the *New Covenant* were devoted to the interdenominational church. I am also perplexed by the absence of reference to the priest or bishop with regard to headship and elders. It would appear that no priest has a leadership role within the Word of God Community at Ann Arbor. The leading priest in South Bend has ceased to attend the meetings of the People of Praise and has formally resigned from the Service Committee, the only executive body in the international movement. In the January 1974 issue of the *New Covenant*, he declared that he was "uneasy about some aspects of the direction which the Service Committee leadership was taking," although he has not left the movement.

As far as I know there is no priest in a leadership position either in South Bend or Ann Arbor. The two theology professors, Dr. William Storey and Dr. Ralph Keifer, and a sociologist, Mrs. Roberta Keifer, associated with the beginning of the movement have withdrawn. They have, however, given witness of outstanding Christian lives and of contributions to renewal, not only in the locality and on the Notre Dame campus, but also in the church as a whole. Both theologians have made invaluable contributions to liturgical and prayer life in America.

LEADERSHIP ROLES

Leadership roles are evolving in an exceedingly interesting manner. From the Core Community, which is comprised of those who have been baptized in the Spirit,[9] is developed a Servant or Pastoral Team. Ralph Martin (Cassette 116) asserts that this is the key leadership group and that it should be small, no more than two to four people altogether. The criteria for belonging to this group are a Christian life, psychological stability, gifts to help people grow, and pastoral heart (a shepherd's heart). The community should discern who is suitable for leadership. Curiously, in the seminar on discernment led by Father O'Connor at the 1971 conference at Notre Dame, there was no mention of priests or bishops taking part in this decision. Although Martin says that there should be flexibility and that the office need not be "life-long," it is interesting to note that leadership has not changed hands either in the Ann Arbor Community or at South Bend.[10] According to Martin, this pastoral team should have weekly meetings.

On his cassette *Growth of the Community Service Group,* Stephen Clark distinguishes between leadership of a prayer meeting and leadership of a community of people. He refers to the apostles' appointing elders and avers that to have an apostle come and teach the community would be the best thing, but that most communities are not in a position to do this. He traces the stages of leadership from informal leadership to a group of people who gather for an additional meeting, such as the Service Group, and states that *the Lord's plan is to have a group through whom he (the Lord) can speak.* Is there a claim here to divine inspiration?

Clark thinks that it is a mistake to divide the responsibilities in the community or to invite others into the group. This makes the Service Group unworkable. He says that the right step is probably to turn the Service Group into a Core Group and for those who have pastoral gifts (two or three persons) to take the overall responsibility. If this is not feasible, a small group becomes a Pastoral Team. The next step is to choose people for functions similar to those in the New Testament which are the province of elders and deacons. The *Report on the Word of God Community* sums up the Pentecostal position on leadership. I quote verbatim:

At the fall conference [1970], it was decided to try to discover the pattern of communal organizations the early Christians had. The leadership structure of the community was modeled on the leadership patterns among the early Christians, because their leadership patterns were fitted for the life of the community.

The heads of the community are the coordinators. The position of coordinator is modeled on the position of elder in the early Christian Communities. The word "elder" is avoided to avoid any claim to be the same as an ordained minister, but the function is similar: the elder is a more mature and respected person[11] within the community who directs the life of the community. The regular direction of the community is carried out by the coordinators as a body. Two coordinators are responsible for the community as a whole and two for each of the subcommunities, except one which has three. The coordinators are assisted by "servants" and "handmaids" of the community. The handmaids of the community are especially responsible for the care of the women in the community. . . .

The principles that have been used to construct the leadership in our community are the same ones that are an increasing concern of the postconciliar Church. We have accepted the principle of the involvement and participation of the whole people[12] in the direction of the life of the community. We have accepted the principle that leadership, especially directive leadership, should always be exercised in a body (collegially). And yet have also preserved the principle that Christian communal life is not democratic in the sense that decisions are made by vote (pp. 9–10).

Conclusion

Type I Pentecostals have worked out an elaborate community structure which depends largely upon the unquestioning submission of the majority to male coordinators.

The system is not without its dangers. The New York *Times* of September 16, 1975, carried a headline, "Charismatic Movement Is Facing Internal Discord over a Teaching Called 'Discipling.'" It described the Neo-Pentecostal movement with its spiritual gifts and referred to a controversial teaching known as discipling. According to this, Pentecostals are divided into groups of about ten under the direction of one male (shepherd). Members obey the shepherd and tithe to him. Sometimes allegiance to the shepherd conflicts with allegiance to one's denominational church. David du Plessis, a Pentecostal minister, sees this as a threat to unity within the movement. However, Derek Prince, an exorcist, defends the teaching which is also supported by Bob Mumford. Prince and Mumford, both ministers of Good News Fellowship, an independent charismatic church in Fort Lauderdale, Florida, are strongly influential in Type I Pentecostalism. The Chicago *Tribune* of October 11, 1975, printed a similar article, entitled " 'Charismatic' Movement Faces Growing Rift." *Logos*, a Pentecostal magazine, has devoted a whole issue to this question. In the May 1975 issue of *Logos*, Charles Farah, Jr., a professor at Oral Roberts University, speaks of denominationalism as a sin (p. 7). He strongly urges discipleship and says that the story of Ananias and Sapphira (Acts 5) "as far as the continuance of purity of the church is concerned, is one of the most important miracles in the whole book of Acts." He expects to see miracles like this occur again. However, he admits that:

extra-local authority could easily lead to extra-local hierarchy, and this is the most serious problem of all. Like Hamlet's father's ghost, there stands waiting in the wings the possibility of a new charismatic denomination. Every piece of the puzzle is in place. Every necessary ingredient is here. There is the extra-local authority, there is recognition of apostles, there is the recognition of discipleship groups as churches and there is the financial structure to support it. National "conventions" are already being held with the speakers carefully screened to make sure they speak only that which is acceptable to one another. The next step could easily be the emergence of the crypto-denomination as a new full blown charismatic denomination (pp. 8–9).

Discipling is of enormous consequence to Catholic Pentecostals. The Charismatic Communication Center is already listing a book by Juan Carlos Ortiz, *Call to Discipleship*. Ortiz also wrote in the issue of *Logos* mentioned above. He believes that we are experiencing the last days (*Call to Discipleship*, p. xi) and advocates a New Testament church (p. xii). He teaches submission to men of God (p. xiv) and emphasizes the priesthood and apostleship of all Christians (pp. 18, 27). He also repudiates democratic principles within the churches (pp. 27, 91–92) and announces that the first step to discipleship is submission (pp. 73–78, 80). Throughout the book runs a strain of anticlericalism, a reflection of Ortiz's feelings about those pastors who are not willing to espouse his tenets on authority, discipleship, and submission. In September 1975 forty-six hundred men, including Catholics, met at the second Men's Shepherds' Conference in Kansas City. Women, except a writer for the *National Catholic Reporter*, were excluded. The *New Covenant* had advertised the conference and listed eleven speakers and prayer leaders and a committee of five. No Catholic priests were in either group, although Stephen Clark, Paul DeCelles, Ralph Martin, and Kevin Ranaghan were listed with fundamentalist ministers such as Don Bashan, a minister of Good News Fellowship; Larry Christenson; Bob Mumford; and Derek Prince. In the last week of August 1976, the Third Men's Shepherds' Conference was scheduled at the University of Notre Dame, Indiana. Three thousand men were expected to attend. No women were to be admitted. This information was procured from the Calendar Office, Center for Continuing Education, University of Notre Dame. The words of Patricia McCarty de Zutter, reporting on the second conference in the October 10, 1975, *National Catholic Reporter*, come to mind: "To me, a better model (than shepherd) comes not from a parable but from the person of Jesus who was willing to risk the pain and pleasure of being with his friends rather than above them."

NOTES

1. One household belonging to the People of Praise Community fasts three times a week.

2. Leaders attended a theological conference held at Benet Lake, Wisconsin, June 1969, and at the Bergamo Center, Dayton, Ohio, in 1968 and 1970. There was also a small meeting in Dallas, Texas, February 1971. The only person to continue theological conferences appears to be Father Edward D. O'Connor, but women theologians were precluded from the first one held in the summer of 1973. Another one was held in the spring of 1974, but the audience was very meager; none of the members of the People of Praise, South Bend, or the Word of God, Ann Arbor, accepted the invitation. One woman responded to a paper, but she is not a Pentecostal and has no lively interest in the subject. However, women were permitted to participate in the dialogue.

3. It would seem that the more organized groups have been influenced by a number of members of the cursillo movement in South Bend. Judging from the cassettes available, most of the main speakers at conferences are from this group of people. They include Stephen Clark; Ralph Martin; Kevin Ranaghan; Kerry Koller; Bert Ghezzi (formerly of the Grand Rapids community, now at Ann Arbor); Paul and Jeanne DeCelles; James Byrne (formerly of South Bend); and Leon and Virginia Kortenkamp (members of the John the Baptist community in San Francisco). I note this because it may be of interest to the historian of the movement.

4. Information concerning this interesting group may be obtained from Mr. and Mrs. Richard Giloth, 1036 West Jefferson Blvd., South Bend, Indiana. At their own request they were not listed in the *Catholic Directory of Prayer Groups* because they understood that the directory was confined to Catholic groups. See their letter in the *National Catholic Reporter* of October 17, 1975.

5. Father John Quinn differs on this point from many of the lay Pentecostal leaders (Quinn's cassette *The Spirit in the Sacraments*). I concur with Father Quinn.

6. The term *gift* is interesting because the Greek word in 2 Tim. 1:6 is *charism*. Most likely this text refers to an ordained minister.

7. For further teaching on these subjects, see the following issues of the *New Covenant*: October 1973, pp. 17–19; December 1973, pp. 3–10; and January 1974, pp. 19–23.

8. The use of the word *installed* in the *Report of the Word of God Community*, p. 5, is interesting. As Daniel Danielson, a Pentecostal priest, describes it in an article in the December 1971 issue of *Sisters Today*, there is a ceremony attached. According to Danielson the officers are "charged by the community for their office in a ceremony analogous to ordination, only without any one leader [bishop]."

9. Entrance into the Core Group is not through the sacrament of baptism but through baptism of the Spirit. Speaking of the weekly meetings of the subcommittees and the gatherings of the whole community, the *Report of the Word of God Community* says, "These are not public meetings, but are for those who have been baptized in the Spirit, and having made some commitment to the community, are invited to attend. There are now almost four hundred in this group" (p. 3). Refer to Ralph Martin's cassette *Pastoral Situations Which Aid Initiation.* He asserts that the Core Group is for those baptized in the Spirit. The Ann Arbor Core Group now has about 14,000 members.

10. The leaders in the Ann Arbor Community are Stephen Clark and Ralph Martin together with James Cavnar and Gerry Rauch. In the *Statement from the Notre Dame–South Bend Service Group Concerning N.*, made in June 1971, the leaders are said to have been functioning since 1967 and "subsequently, these same people have been formally ratified by the community as its leaders" (p. 4).

11. The Pentecostals seem to measure maturity by the length of time since one's baptism in the Spirit, but very little or no recognition seems to be given to those who have lived a committed life to Christ for many years outside the Pentecostal community.

12. I cannot understand the reference to the "whole people" since, apparently, women are omitted from decisions and there is no reference to a priest or bishop.

2

Recent Discussions
of Type I Pentecostals

The material used in the preceding chapter was taken from Pentecostal sources. In 1975 certain criticisms of the communities came to the fore. When William G. Storey, professor of church history and one of the founding fathers of the movement both at Duquesne University and the University of Notre Dame, was interviewed by A.D. *Correspondence* on September 14, 1972, he saw Pentecostalism as a healthy, integrated prayer movement within the church. He found the leadership "generally intelligent, informed, dedicated and free from a cult of personality" and open to guidance from the church. But when he was interviewed again on May 24, 1975, Storey was apprehensive about the direction the Pentecostal movement was taking. He found forms of worship that were disconsonant with the Catholic tradition. He saw difficulties in the ecumenical bridges of reconciliation, one of literature and one of community. He felt that the theological positions of some of the literature distributed by the national leaders could not be reconciled with Catholic doctrine.

For conformation of this point, see Fichter's *The Catholic Cult of the Paraclete* (pp. 28–37). He lists such tenets dissonant with Catholic tradition as rebaptism, delivery from demons, rejection of hierarchical priesthood, exaggerated emphasis on Scripture, teaching that *dulia* (devotion to the saints) and *hyperdulia* (devotion to Mary) is idolatry, a belief in eternal security (which he calls personal salvation) and in the conviction that the Spirit speaks to the heart, not to the mind. Storey discerned dangers in authoritarianism, especially in the area of coercion of consciences, and he spoke of "an invasion of the internal forum which Catholics identify with the privacy of the confessional." He reproached the leadership for suppressing dissent and criticism and spoke about the screening of the books and tape recordings that are sold at the Communications Center in South Bend. When traveling around the country Storey had observed a growing focus on the life of the community itself, including "an entire revelation of a person's whole life process to his immediate superiors." Storey expressed deep concern about manifestation of conscience, confession of sin before several community leaders, and files of people's personal sins and approved priests and confessors. He was also concerned about fundamentalism. Storey concluded by stating that he would like to see an investigating commission which would include professional persons such as canon lawyers and psychologists, as well as theologians.

On May 30, 1975, in his *Statement On Behalf of the Catholic Charismatic Renewal Service Committee,* Ranaghan replied to Storey's criticisms. He stated that the movement was unstructured and diverse, that the Service Committee had dealt with faulty teaching in a responsible manner, and that they would welcome constructive criticism. He objected strongly to any mention of schism and averred that the "overwhelming majority of participants and leaders are deeply, personally and totally committed to the Catholic Church." He repudiated Storey's statement that the National Service Committee was a small, closed group of persons. He denied any dilemma about the Eucharist. He claimed that Benjamin Zablocki's book *The Joyful Community* had little influence on Pentecostal community life. In response to Ranaghan I have already quoted Fichter concerning the organization of the movement (*The Catholic Cult of the Paraclete*, pp. 35–38). Fichter's statistics on heterodoxy should be noted. In the Midwest 67 percent of lay charismatics lean toward unorthodox doctrines; in the East, 55 percent (p. 48). With regard to obedience to bishops, Fichter finds that newcomers to the prayer groups "are twice as likely (60%) as the old-timers (30%)" to say that they would continue to hold meetings if the bishop prohibited them (pp. 78, 104). Fichter (p. 116) quotes DeCelles, who has come out on the side of ecclesiastical disobedience in the *New Covenant*. Fichter claims that he represents 45 percent of the Pentecostals. Concerning *The Joyful Community* Fichter comments that Pentecostals feel a longing for community which may explain "the popularity of Zablocki's account of the Bruderhof among them" (p. 100). Thus it would seem that Ranaghan's findings differ from the sociologist's.

The Storey interview led to further revelations. It inspired Rick Casey to write six articles in the *National Catholic Reporter*. Casey described in detail the True House, a now defunct Christian community in South Bend. In the first article he paid special attention to the breakthrough ministry. This comprised sustained interrogation of community members, often in three late-night sessions; general confession in the presence of the coordinators and the Roman rite of exorcism. Details of people's sins and weaknesses were often kept on file (*National Catholic Reporter*, 15 August 1975, pp. 1–2; NCR, 29 August 1975, pp. 4 and 10). The local bishop was not informed about such practices. Casey dealt with the question of headship and submission and the careful screening of all teaching media.

Members of True House traveled widely giving seminars on community and were very influential throughout the United States. In confirmation of this, *True House Covenant Commentary* (a mimeographed circular) states:

IV. . . .
The coordinators have an overall responsibility for the life of the True House and *its public ministry, as well as its regional and national ministries* [italics mine].

In *The Catholic Cult of the Paraclete* (p. 36) Fichter also refers to the national leaders traveling about the country on lecture tours.

In his September 5, 1975, *National Catholic Reporter* article, Casey described the Word of God Community, Ann Arbor, Michigan, which is one of the estimated twenty to forty covenanted communities around the country. The community is modeled on the New Testament, but the leaders are called coordinators, not elders. The Word of God has seventy-five households and its own hierarchy. The head-coordinators are Stephen Clark, Ralph Martin and Bruce Yocum, one of the coordinators of the Ann Arbor Word of God Community. There is a brotherhood of twelve persons, eleven coordinators, and seventy-five heads. There are fourteen hundred members in the Word of God. The doctrine that is given the greatest emphasis is headship and submission wherein members place their whole lives under the directions of the heads. Faults, such as coming late for dinner, are attributed to a spirit of rebelliousness. People are afraid of their heads, who are becoming aloof from the membership and often make decisions without consulting others. Punishments are imposed; for example, unpunctuality might be punished by forcing the member to go to bed an hour early for a week. In some cases heads have told people not to go to confession, but recently a memorandum was sent round correcting this.

In his September 12, 1975, article for the *National Catholic Reporter,* Casey dealt with structure in the movement. The People of Praise and the Word of God are two divisions of one cooperation. Casey states, "Ann Arbor acts roughly as a production arm . . . while South Bend serves as a retailer." The Communications Center in South Bend mails its catalogs to eighty-three thousand persons. Casey remarks, "No material is included which disagrees with the major teachings of the movement as determined by Steve Clark and other leaders here [Ann Arbor]."

A Good Shepherd Program provides books for prayer meetings throughout the country. Again, the leaders decide which items will be on the tables. Prayer groups are given not only books but "a manual on inventory, accounting, sales tax and how to keep the Internal Revenue Service off their backs."

The *New Covenant,* the Pentecostal magazine, is not an open forum but represents the current positions of the leaders. Phil O'Mara of the Word of God community is the book review editor; he receives a list of approved books for review.

Ann Arbor and South Bend also supervise the regional conferences, where both talks and prophecies are carefully screened. The two communities train prayer group leaders throughout the country, and apparently speakers are given outlines of their talks by Stephen Clark. They write them out in full and submit them to Clark for approval.

Thus there seems to be minute control through the whole Pentecostal power structure. Casey finds it frightening in its "anti-intellectual fundamentalism, and frightening in its growing strain of militarism" (*National Catholic Reporter,* 29 September 1975, pp. 1–2). This power structure responds to deprivation on various levels and becomes an answer to both important and insignificant questions. However, Casey is incorrect when he states that the national leaders have avoided the abuses that occurred at True House. The breakthrough ministry began with those who are now on the Service Committee. *The Life in the Spirit Seminars Team Manual*, to be discussed below, provides for a special team of people who gather detailed information from candidates and transfer this in writing to their superiors.

Casey refers to Father Healey's comparison between the Roman crowd hailing Mussolini with "Duce, Duce, Duce" and the Pentecostal enthusiasm for their leaders. The parallel is apt. Neither must one forget the important role of music in swaying a crowd toward one leader or the other. Casey notes the military language recently used by Ralph Martin. In the September 5, 1975, issue of the *National Catholic Reporter* Catherine Haven reports Martin saying that "it is imperative that charismatics 'know who our brothers are and who our enemies are.'" This statement indicates a strange polarity in the heart of a former conscientious objector. In his September 29, 1975, article for the *National Catholic Reporter*, Casey also quotes Ralph Martin as having said: "I can see more and more how our community and many other communities and Christians are being prepared to take part with Jesus in the coming spiritual warfare, functioning with the effectiveness of an army." Casey ends his series of articles with the pregnant words: "So the Prince of Peace, who would not be king, is now being fashioned a general. This is the stuff from which crusades are made. And crusades have not been among Christianity's finest hours."

Type I Pentecostals' response to these criticisms was disappointing. Their statements were either too generalized—weakly defended denials of the allegations made against them—or consisted of pious exhortations (*National Catholic Reporter*, 5 September 1975, p. 14; 17 October 1975, pp. 9–11, 14). None of the leaders replied with concrete suggestions for amending any of the undesirable characteristics of the movement. The most responsible letter was written by Father Constantine-Paul

Michael Belisarius, S.J., from Canada. He recommended that leaders be more human, more open to humor and a sense of playfulness. He encouraged the Pentecostals not to dodge behind clichés or to put their faith in gurus but to bear uncompromising witness and have trust in God.

3

Initiation

Catholic Neo-Pentecostal groups and communities have established a regular initiation catechumenate, which culminates in prayers for the baptism of the Spirit and which is, apparently, the only way[1] of gaining entrance into the Core Community and full participation in the Charismatic Renewal Community. Ralph Martin in *As the Spirit Leads Us* (edited by Kevin and Dorothy Ranaghan) speaks against "mixed groups" and floaters, that is, those who have no regular commitment to the meeting. He states specifically that the presence of non-Charismatic people "deactivates" (pp. 153–55) the group. The only people who seem to·be exempt from the catechumenate are those who entered before the arrangements were fully sealed.

On his cassette *Christian Initiation*, Ralph Martin describes initiation as "that process by which people are brought to a new life in Jesus Christ in the body of Christ." He sees the necessity (not the variable choice) of linking this initiation organically with a growing Christian community. He does refer to the sacraments as the primary Christian initiation and does speak of contemporary efforts to make sacramental life more vital, but he seems to have little confidence in these attempts at renewal.

He speaks of the necessity, not only for the renewal of the sacraments, but for a new context for the sacraments. This he sees in (1) the catechumenate and (2) the full Christian community, a living body of Christ. Both of these he seems to identify with Neo-Pentecostalism.

Martin then proceeds to make a complete analogy with the early Christian initiation process: the elements of *kerygma* (basic gospel message), repentance, *didache* (teaching), a sponsorship, and being part of one body. He speaks of "those who are entering" (not having entered) this body. He notes that in the early church the catechumenate had a definite end, which was also a public act. Hence, he argues, the Pentecostal initiation should follow the same pattern. Indeed, the Pentecostal initiation does repeat Christian initiation with two exceptions. Pentecostal initiation is conducted by lay people. There is no mention of priests taking part in the initiation process either in Ralph Martin's talk or in the statements of others who address themselves to this question. Pentecostal "baptism" is not by water but through the imposition of hands and prayer. It is true that in theory those responsible for the Life in the Spirit Seminars, which is the catechumenate, confess that they believe that the sacrament of baptism confers the Holy Spirit. However, the *Report on the Word of God Community* at Ann Arbor (pp. 6–7), in describing how one becomes part of the community, speaks clearly of a candidate coming to the seminars and beginning to hear "how he can receive the Holy Spirit and live this new Christian Life." One of the most popular books and recommended reading given to these candidates is Stephen Clark's *Baptized in the Spirit*. It states:

. . . the descriptions of people receiving the Spirit in Acts show that the people involved did not receive the Spirit until after they had turned to Christ, believed in him, and been baptized. . . . [the author is referring to Acts 19:1–7] Luke [who wrote Acts] seems anxious to emphasize that it was the laying on of hands which was the reason for the coming of the Spirit on them, *not baptism* [italics mine].

The same thing is true in the eighth chapter of Acts. The account of how the people in the Samaritan town received the Spirit seemed to be designed to emphasize the fact that it was *not baptism but the laying on of hands which gave the Spirit* . . . [italics mine].

In other words, in both passages, receiving the Holy Spirit came *subsequently* [italics mine] to believing and being baptized. The difference between being joined to Christ and receiving the Spirit is confirmed in passages in the New Testament which mention the two in a parallel but separate way (pp. 52–53).

Clark then cites Titus 3:5 and John 3:5.

Clark seems, inadvertently, to have non-Roman Catholic teaching in the above, namely, that the Spirit does not come with baptism but with an infilling through subsequent imposition of hands. Mainline Pentecostals vary in their opinions concerning whether the reception of the Spirit is a two-step or a three-step process. However, the Catholic church teaches that the fullness of the Holy Spirit is given in the sacrament of baptism. The text from Acts 8 is difficult, and, although scholars have various interpretations, the best is that of F. E. Bruner, which he gives in his book A *Theology of the Holy Spirit*:

It was evidently not the divine plan, according to Luke's understanding, that the first church outside Jerusalem should arise entirely without apostolic contact. For this to have occurred could have indicated the indifference of the apostolic tradition—viz., of the history of Jesus Christ—and of the unity of the church. Both the tradition and the union were preserved through the apostolic visitation. The Samaritans were not left to become an isolated sect with no bonds of union with the apostolic church in Jerusalem. If a Samaritan church and a Jewish church had arisen independently, side by side, without the dramatic removal of the ancient and bitter barriers of prejudice between the two, particularly at the level of ultimate authority, the young church of God would have been in schism from the inception of its mission. The drama of the Samaritan affair in Acts 8 included among its purposes the vivid and visual dismantling of the wall of enmity between Jew and Samaritan and the preservation of the precious unity of the church of God through the unique divine "interception" and then prompt presentation of the Spirit in the presence of the apostles (p. 176).

Thus the Samaritan Pentecost is a very unusual case and may not be quoted as a precedent. Further, a correct interpretation of the Greek text of Titus 3:5 and John 3:5 does not support the contention that being joined to Christ and receiving the Spirit are two different events.

The Life in the Spirit Seminars

A definite catechism and instruction manual is used by most Type I communities. The instruction is conducted over a period of six weeks like the original Lenten catechumenate. It is described in detail in *The Life in the Spirit Seminars Team Manual.* The Life in the Spirit Seminars are a series of seminars explaining the basic Christian message and culminating in the release of the Spirit. The *Team Manual* is now in its third edition, and more than seventy thousand copies have been sold. It has been translated into Korean, Chinese, French, Dutch, Spanish, Italian, and Sotho, a Bantu language spoken in South Africa. The accompanying booklet, *Finding New Life,* which is provided for the candidates, has sold more than two hundred fifty thousand copies.

In the *Team Manual* the talks are not sacramentally oriented. For example, there is no adequate discussion of baptism. There is also insufficient reference to confirmation and no mention of the sacrament of penance although repentance is stressed and the Eucharist receives one passing, superficial reference. This is disappointing since study of the seminar program reveals many possibilities for sacramental orientation. For example, the first three talks would easily fit in with the contemporary teaching on the three sacraments of baptism, confirmation, and penance, respectively. Father John Quinn, on his cassette *The Spirit and the Sacraments*, makes a very valuable contribution on this point. In the *Manual* there is no mention of the priest's role. The team leader holds a key position. The *Manual* portends that these groups are building up their own liturgy or quasi-sacramental system rather than using the liturgical and sacramental system of the church. While the *Manual* professes to be denominationally indifferent or, as the writer expresses it, "universal" in its orientation (p. 7), there is no reason why it should not have sections, perhaps in small print, for Roman Catholics and other members of the sacramental churches.

The seminars seek ". . . to bypass all dogmatic or theological questions and reach directly to a person's heart. . . . Serious theological issues are usually best taken care of outside of the seminars and not in them" (p. 8). However, the denominational indifference is a matter of concern; in fact, the U.S. bishops have specifically stated that this was one cause of anxiety with reference to the Neo-Pentecostal movement in the Roman Catholic community (*Origins*, June 1972, pp. 60–61).

The *Life in the Spirit Seminars Team Manual* appears to be influenced by Douglas Hyde's *Dedication and Leadership: Learning From the Communists*, a popular book sold by the Charismatic Renewal Services and listed in a bibliography composed by Paul DeCelles for studying community. Hyde, a member of the Communist Party for twenty years, resigned as the news editor of the London *Daily Worker* in 1948. Shortly after, he renounced communism and, with his wife and children, joined the Catholic church. In his book Hyde describes the techniques of Communist training; at the beginning of the book he states that he will discuss "those Communist leadership training methods which are capable of imitation or adaptation by Christians" (p. 9).

It is a serious question, however, whether Communist methods can or should be imitated by Christians. I do not think that Communist methods can be completely separated from Communist goals and applied to Christian goals. Pentecostals who attempt this are likely to find that the Communist methods will eat up the Christian goals. The group dynamics and manipulation of the individual that are a part of the Communist technique might well hinder the deep yet quiet working of the Spirit. A Pentecostal group might be able to change the outer behavior of an initiate by behavior-changing techniques, but that is something different from the transforming work of the Spirit. It is folly to think that we can enhance the Spirit by adapting Communist leadership training methods. What has Pentecost to do with November 1917?

Tongues

Dr. John Kildahl, in his book *The Psychology of Speaking in Tongues*, discusses the real possibility that tongue-speakers are under a sort of hypnosis and are subordinate to the authority figure who introduces them to tongues. In light of this one becomes concerned about the emphasis placed on the gift of tongues in the Ann Arbor–South Bend type of Pentecostalism. In the first edition of the *Team Manual* there were more than thirty references to tongues in 101 pages. In the second edition it is even more strongly emphasized. The *Manual* appears to equate baptism of the Spirit and tongues in several places, or at least thinks of them together (*Team Manual*, pp. 6 8, 20, 27). The *Manual* rules that a team member should have yielded to tongues himself: "It is very difficult for someone who has not yielded to the gift of tongues to help someone else to do so" (*Team Manual*, pp. 26, 116, 145). The team leader teaches the people to sing in tongues. They do so in a chorus together. He also exhorts them to pray in tongues every day. (It is interesting that tongues is advocated every day but not a daily Eucharist.) If someone has not prayed in tongues, the team leader coaxes him or her to do so (*Team Manual*, p. 152). Those who make babbling sounds are encouraged to continue so that this may evolve into tongues (*Team Manual*, pp. 151, 157). Tongues is seen as a very important, one might even say an essential, gift (*Team Manual*, pp. 61, 72, 77, 148–49).[2] The commitment prayer that recipients are encouraged to say includes a direct petition to God for the gift of tongues (*Team Manual*, p. 152; *Finding New Life in the Spirit*, p. 23). *Finding New Life in the Spirit* is a small booklet prepared by the Charismatic Renewal and used by candidates in the Life in the Spirit Seminars.

It would seem that tongues are of very special importance to the Ann Arbor–South Bend type of Pentecostals. Their stress on this gift together with various techniques they employ to induce tongues and their emphasis on the importance of the authority figure do present an enormous risk of hypnosis followed by regression of the ego and personality transference. My advice would be to abstain from this emphasis and these techniques and also to refrain from praying over people for tongues. I feel that conferring the gift of tongues should be left entirely to the Holy Spirit. Although I do believe there is a genuine gift of tongues bestowed by God without human intervention, it is also my belief that one should not go so far as to say that "if you are unwilling to receive the gift of tongues, you are putting a block on the Lord's work and the Holy Spirit will not be free to work fully in you" (*Finding New Life in the Spirit*, p. 23).

Just as the catechumenate has become more highly developed in Type I Pentecostalism during the last two or three years, so the idea of community has become more concrete. After the Life in the Spirit Seminars the candidate attends additional lectures known as Growth Seminars or Christian Living Seminars. Then, if deemed fit, he or she enters on a novitiate for approximately one year or two (a year's novitiate, during which no dating is permitted, is required by the People of Praise) and finally makes a formal covenant and submits his or her life to the overall coordinators. The form of the covenant differs with each community. The book that appears to be most influential in the formation of community is Zablocki's *The Joyful Community*. The author is a sociologist and is not a member of this Hutterian community. The account is unbiased, and the quotations Zablocki cites are taken from statements of members and ex-members. The book is sold by the Pentecostals and, to my knowledge, has received no negative criticism from them.

Zablocki describes the Hutterite movement as having originated with a group of charismatics in Germany in 1920 and traveled through the stages of "communion," "charismatic community," "transitional community," "isolated sect," communitarian social movement, and thence to a church—community. During these stages it left Germany, came to America, and affiliated with the Hutterian (strict Anabaptist) sect. A somewhat analogous development has taken place in Type I Catholic Pentecostalism but in a much shorter period, probably because of the help of modern communications media and the creation of a good public image, which masks the elements that may not be in harmony with the tenets of the Catholic church. Type I Pentecostalist communities bear affinity to the Hutterite community in the following respects. Communal sharing is practiced in varying degrees. Both have a similar ideology of marriage and the family although all the children belong to one generation in the Catholic Pentecostal movement.[3] The united or uniform brotherhood is very powerful,[4] one Pentecostal group has ruled that they "have authority to exclude from their open and general meeting those who do not accept their theology."[5] I have learned through private conversations with the parish priest whose property they use that the group has implemented this decision against his will. The leading priest no longer attends these meetings. The leadership, control of members, and elimination of even minor dissent is parallel in both the Pentecostal and the Hutterite brotherhoods. Both practice exclusion and have a penal system. Zablocki's chapter "On Leaving the Old Self Behind" shows many features that are appearing in the Life in the Spirit Seminars and the teaching and practice within Type I groups. Public confession in covenant communities is fairly common (pp. 257–58).

It is extremely enlightening to read Zablocki's book, and it is important to do so because it shows how people with upright intention and deeply sincere faith can be led into situations which are not consonant with the teachings of the Gospel. I have attempted to show another example of this in my essay "Pentecostal Blueprint," which appears in *Baptism of the Spirit*. Here I describe the Qumran Covenanters' community, situated by the Dead Sea in the first century B.C. and first century A.D., which changed from a charismatic group to a highly structured, hierarchical, penal, and exclusive community. I contrast this with the early church of the New Testament, which became more and more inclusive, forgiving, and socially conscious. The reports of Storey and Casey, discussed in Chapter 2, suggest to me that Type I is moving in the Qumran direction.

NOTES

1. I do not know another way of entering the Core Community, but I am unable to say whether entry into the Core Community always involves a covenant commitment. Recently I received information that entry into the Core Community is preceded by two seminar courses and a short trial period.

2. *Team Manual*, pp. 61, 72, 77, 114, 115, 126, 131, 136, 144, 147. ("Everyone should want the gift of tongues, it is a gift of God" [p. 150]. "If you did not speak in tongues tonight, expect it to come soon" [p. 152].) At the concluding team meeting, among the questions discussed are: "Did any not find a new re-

lationship with the Lord (did any not make a commitment to him, not pray in tongues, not want to be part of the community/prayer group?)" (p. 171).

3. See Zablocki, *The Joyful Community*, pp. 127–30. The Pentecostals have not yet adopted distinctive dress. However, serious discussion concerning the veiling of women at prayer meetings arose at the leaders' meeting held at Ann Arbor in January 1974. Four priests rose to defend the women, but it is reported that their statements were ruled out of order by the lay leaders. Dorothy Ranaghan, on the cassette *Roles of Men and Women*, says that the Pentecostals are waiting for "authority teaching" concerning women and blue jeans!

4. *The Joyful Community*, pp. 152–86, but especially pp. 170–171; concerning attraction for the opposite sex, pp. 173–76; the public questioning and accusation, pp. 178–86; the self—and world —rejection, p. 181: "For the initiate, the final stage of ego loss comes with baptism."

5. See *The Joyful Community*, pp. 153–54, where absolute unity (uniformity) is required before prayer at the *Gemeindestunde* is commenced, that is, no one must dissent from the leaders.

4

Catholic Neo-Pentecostalism
and the Radical Reformation

In 1971 it became increasingly apparent to me that South Bend–Ann Arbor Neo-Pentecostalism had, without consciously intending to do so, modeled itself upon a theology not dissimilar to that of the Radical Reformation. Anabaptist or, to speak more precisely, Hutterian, patterns are now significant in Type I Pentecostalism. This fact is confirmed by the movement's listing and selling Zablocki's book *The Joyful Community* and by its modeling community leadership according to principles found therein, although different titles are used for officers. These principles include a strong and rigid hierarchy to whom obedience is required, a nonprofessional teaching body which purports to speak directly through the inspiration of the Spirit, a complicated exclusion system, the subordination of women, and withdrawal from the world.[1] The prayer group has developed from a *koinonia* (community) to an *ecclesiola* (little church) (Fichter, *The Catholic Cult of the Paraclete*, p. 37).

Cultural Conditioning

Charismatic movements have always been a product of their cultural environment. Norman Cohn observes that it has always been the lot of the common people, when they have grown dissatisfied with church, state, or society, to await a *propheta* who would bind them together into a group, which often emerges "as a movement of a peculiar kind, driven on by wild enthusiasm born of desperation" (*The Pursuit of the Millennium*, p. 315). Moreover, this "desperation" is aggravated when people feel and suffer alienation from the church. Their need for the church is shown by the eagerness with which they welcome ascetic reform and accept and even adore[2] the charismatic leader. Because of the emotional needs of the deprived, whether in material or spiritual well-being, social movements become surrogates for the church, and often these "salvationist groups" are led by miracle workers (p. 316). So it was in the sixteenth century when in addition to social and economic unrest, Luther caused anxieties as a result of his stand against the church. The laxity and degenerate practices of its clergy created additional discontent. There arose a group of people who were both perturbed and disorientated but who found themselves unable to side with Luther or the Catholic church. Against this historical background the Anabaptist movement arose.

Anabaptism cannot be identified with the enthusiastic and often apocalyptic and millenarian movements. Similarly, Catholic Neo-Pentecostalism is for the most part much more restrained and reserved than mainline Pentecostalism. Speaking of Anabaptism, George Williams avers in his book *The Radical Reformation*:

. . . one seems to see beneath the lifted weight of centuries of ecclesiastical domination a squirming, spawning, nihilistic populace of its own, confused by the new theological terms of predestination, faith alone, *Gelassenheit* (self-possession), and by the new Biblical texts seized upon with an almost maniacal glare. It is hard to find anything in common between this phase of St. Gall Anabaptism and the sober fervor and evangelical zeal of Grebel, Mantz and Blaurock (pp. 133–34).

Indeed, people welcomed the "uncompromising message of the Brethren," and Anabaptist teaching attracted those of pious and upright lives (p. 132). The Radical Reformers gathered together and disciplined a "true church" (*rechte Kirche*) which they modeled upon their perception of the apostolic pattern in the biblical text (Littell, *The Anabaptist View of the Church,* pp. xvii). The *Schärmer* (enthusiasts) were the uncontrolled element of Reform while the Anabaptists were the orderly and disciplined element.

Today's Type I Catholic Neo-Pentecostal movement is a product of a similar cultural atmosphere. The charismatic movement arose in the United States in the aftermath of Vatican II with its deemphasis of authoritarianism and the resulting tendency to permissiveness. New theological concepts became popular, as well as a new pluralism, both legitimate and illegitimate, within the church. The charismatic movement sprung up amidst a mood of insecurity and "desperation" felt by many religious men and women. Unsettling circumstances such as an unstable and disintegrating political situation, the drug culture, an increasing divorce rate, and the disruption of family life drove people to seek some stabilizing force in their lives. Many found it in Type I Neo-Pentecostalism. Type I Pentecostals not only paint a black picture of the world at large,[3] but stress the failure of church renewal and the success of the Pentecostals' own endeavors.[4] They openly teach that "normal church life is not enough" (*Team Manual,* p. 160) and that Christian community is not optional but mandatory[5] if one is truly to live "the"[6] life in the Holy Spirit. Thus a somewhat similar background is shared by Catholic Neo-Pentecostalism and its predecessor, Anabaptism.

Early Beginnings

As we have indicated, some trace the beginning of Anabaptism to the spiritualist and apocalyptic movements that directly preceded it. But it seems more likely that Anabaptism arose as a reaction against these movements and that it originated among university educated men such as Conrad Grebel and Menno Simons and the groups of less-educated lay people who met in their houses to study the Sacred Text. As Cohn states in *The Pursuit of the Millennium,* the reformers had appealed to the Bible and thus opened it to lay people, who gave interpretations of it according to their personal divine promptings (p. 272). This was the beginning of Anabaptism in Switzerland. Thus from 1522 to 1523 there were house meetings for Bible study, and biblical radicalism arose among the common people (Littell, *The Anabaptist View of the Church,* p. 11). In *The Radical Reformation,* George Williams describes how the first evangelists met in private homes, then in the guild hall of the tailors, then in that of the weavers, then on the second floor of the Metzge, which accommodated one thousand people (p. 128). It was common to meet in the evening for Bible reading and discussion.

In a similar way Vatican II and the introduction into the liturgy, not only of English, but also of the new triennial cycle of lectionary readings, brought the Bible to Catholic lay men and women, and the biblical movement progressed. Like the Anabaptist movement, Neo-Pentecostalism originated in university circles, particularly at a retreat organized by two laymen at Duquesne University. The February 1973 issue of the *New Covenant* is devoted to the origins of the movement which spread to South Bend, Indiana, and to East Lansing and Ann Arbor, Michigan. Eventually the houses became too small, and meetings took place on the University of Notre Dame campus and later in churches in South Bend. The general meeting at Ann Arbor, Michigan, now draws about two thousand people, and, as reported earlier, the *Directory of Catholic Charismatic Prayer Groups* of June 1974 lists some three thousand prayer meetings of varying sizes and composition.

The Idea of the Church

Mass was abolished in Strasburg in 1529, but the complete constitution of the Anabaptist church did not take place until 1534 (Littell, *The Anabaptist View of the Church*, p. 27). Indeed, among early Anabaptists there was at first no clearly defined doctrine of the church. But there were prophets and biblicists, anti-Trinitarians, covenanters, and so on, and the early Anabaptists severed their loose association with the other Reformers and acquired their own pattern of discipline and integrity (p. 3).

Norman Cohn suggests that there were about forty independent sects grouped around charismatic leaders. In these sects little attention was paid either to theological speculation or to formal religious observance. Rather, reliance was placed upon "inner Revelation." Many Anabaptists came from the class of small farmers and hired help or peasants and artisans rather than from the wealthier families (Williams, *The Radical Reformation*, p. 122; and Cohn, *The Pursuit of the Millennium*, p. 275).

Catholic Neo-Pentecostalism also began as a prayer movement with little organization (see chap. 1, pp. 4–5), but neither movement remained unstructured for long. Pilgrim Marpeck criticized the spiritualizing and individualistic thrust of the Reformers as well as the medieval parish system, which the Reformers were loath to abandon (Littell, *The Anabaptist View of the Church*, p. 25). The Radicals, however, said that Luther "tore down the old house, but built no new one in its place" and that Zwingli "threw down all infirmities as with thunder strokes, but erected nothing better in its place" (p. 2). The Radical Reformers conceived of the church as a concrete, disciplined community, and, as Littell declares, "togetherness" was the constant refrain of the brotherhood (Phil. 2:1; 2 Cor. 13:13) (Littell, *The Free Church*, p. 11). Berndt Rothmann (*ca.*

1494–1535), originally with Luther, later turned to Zwingli but ultimately joined the Radical parties to gather "the believers in a holy community separated from the unbelieving godless" (Littell, *The Anabaptist View of the Church*, p. 30).[7] Menno Simons brought the congregations together and formed them into a "permanent association of Anabaptist churches" (p. 40). On his deathbed Menno said that there was nothing so precious to him as the True Church (p. 41).

Among many features of the Anabaptist view of the church, two stand out prominently: (1) the church must be a voluntary association with its spirit and discipline emanating from those who belong to the fellowship and (2) it must follow the New Testament model with regard to faith and organizational pattern (p. 46). Thus by the second decade inspired leadership had largely disappeared, and organizational and creedal conformity were enforced. Elders and synods were the agencies for maintaining church discipline according to the New Testament pattern (p. 37). The Radicals modeled their church on Acts 2, 3, and 4 and embraced communal social organization in various ways and with varying degrees of strictness (pp. 38, 58). Some form of communalism was mandatory because it was deemed to be the life-style for the normative period of the church (p. 59). This idea of restitution of the New Testament church model represented a concerted effort to reverse history and to overthrow power and intellectual sophistication, both of which were felt to adulterate the faith of the church founders. What mattered to the Radicals was apostolicity rather than apostolic succession (p. 80). In *The Recovery of the Anabaptist Vision*, G. P. Herschberger quotes Philip Schaff as having said, "The reformers aimed to reform the old Church by the Bible; the radical attempted to build a new Church from the Bible" (p. 119). Indeed, the real issue between the Reformers and the Radicals was not the act of baptism but two mutually exclusive concepts of the church, namely, the state church and parish system or the restored apostolic church. The Reformers still believed in the church for the masses, the *Volkskirche*. Although Luther had thought of entering the names of earnest Christians in a special book and letting them meet separately from the nominal Christians, and Zwingli had entertained a similar idea, neither man brought his plan to fruition (pp. 40–41). But the Radicals formed a concrete community and kept a book of baptisms, which may have been the first covenant book of believers (Littell, *The Anabaptist View of the Church,* p. 30).

The Anabaptists placed great emphasis upon personal conversion and regeneration, and upon these principles they gathered believers from the national degenerate churches. They were not concerned about the size of their church but refused to compromise with the world and were prepared to break radically with fifteen hundred years of history and culture so that they could return to the New Testament (Herschberger, ed., *The Recovery of the Anabaptist Vision,* pp. 37, 41). Their church, beyond the two distinctive features mentioned above, was founded upon "Christianity as discipleship, the church as a brotherhood, and a new ethic of love (and nonresistance)" (p. 42).

In order to implement these principles the Anabaptists chose to bring their entire lives under the lordship of Christ and to secure this by a covenant of discipleship. Dietrich Philips described the community as the New Jerusalem, and among the community's twelve distinguishing marks he said that it could be "called a city for the reason that as in a city there must be concord; the citizens must hold firmly together, living and conducting themselves according to the same polity, law, and statutes, if the city is to continue" (Williams, ed., *Spiritual and Anabaptist Writers,* p. 255 n.).

The theology of community in Type I Catholic Neo-Pentecostalism resembles that of the Radicals, even in the use of some images and metaphors, although with Type I the "baptism of the Spirit" together with the initial evidence of speaking in tongues (*Team Manual,* pp. 20, 27) takes the place of believers' baptism with water and the Spirit. It has been demonstrated that Kevin Ranaghan[8] and his colleagues see the creation of a concrete community as a natural consequence of "baptism in the Spirit"; that Ralph Martin and others aver that we are in an eschatological, perhaps even apocalyptic, age;[9] that Koller goes so far as to say that it is God's plan to form a church;[10] that Randall is not alone in modeling Pentecostal leadership on the pastoral Epistles (Cassette 156), thus creating a paraecclesial structure.[11]

The development of community and covenant life has been described (Cassette 121), and it would seem that strict discipline is practiced in Type I living situations; this is the Pentecostals' concept of love.[12] The responsibility of bestowing "love" is placed especially on the shoulders of the heads of households and the elders of communities. One may compare Dietrich Philips (Williams, ed., *Spiritual and Anabaptist Writers,* p. 248–49) speaking of the fifth ordinance, the command of love:

But this is true brotherly love, that our chief desire is one another's salvation, by our fervent prayers to God, by Scriptural instruction, admonition, and rebuke, that thereby we may instruct him who is overtaken in a fault, in order to win his soul. And all this we do with Christian patience (Gal. 6:23; 2 Thess. 1:11; James 5:19; 1 John 5:16) having forbearance toward the weak and not simply pleasing ourselves (pp. 248–49).

Earlier I spoke of the fact that the *Team Manual* ends by referring to one who withdraws from the talks and applies to such individuals the text of James 5:19–20, which discusses saving the soul of a sinner.

Type I Catholic Neo-Pentecostalism, like the Radical Reformers, has modeled its community on the pattern of the early church and has established a paraecclesial hierarchy which appears to claim to have "the Key of David," that is, the true understanding of Scripture. In the last part of this chapter we shall see that Type I Neo-Pentecostals also claim the "Key of Peter" (binding and loosing, i.e., disciplinary and excommunication rights). They are gathering earnest Christians who are obliged to pass successfully through the Life in the Spirit Seminars, a form of cathechumenate, and then enter a specific community. The names of these people are entered, not in a baptismal book, but upon commitment cards, which are filed together with personal and, it seems, intimate information about the candidates (*Team Manual*, pp. 181–83). Type I usually rejects a mixed assembly, that is, a group where Pentecostals and "ordinary" Christians pray together. The People of Praise Covenant Community now has doorkeepers established at the entrances to the meeting place to question strangers and to keep out those "who will not accept the theology of the leaders." The "theology" is fundamentalist. Like the Anabaptists, the distinguishing mark of Type I is personal conversion and "new life," which is obtained by passing through the catechumenate (Cassette 109) of the Life in the Spirit Seminars and the *didache* of the Growth Seminars or the Seminars in Christian Living. As did the Anabaptists, Type I Pentecostals regard the church as at least partly degenerate. The *Team Manual* asserts that those who have been turned off by a traditional, rigid form of church life or, on the other hand, by a secularized Christianity which emphasized loving but deemphasized Christ will find "something different in the Life in the Spirit Seminars" (p. 99). This seems to be a somewhat overconfident statement. Perhaps it would be better merely to say: "There are many ways of experiencing authentic Christianity, and the Life in the Spirit Seminars may provide you with one."

Thus, although Kevin Ranaghan delivered a talk entitled "The Lord, the Spirit, and the Church" (*New Covenant*, August 1972, pp. 1–5), at the Sixth International Conference, which was quite consonant with the ecclesiology of the Roman Catholic communion, and offered a most commendable program for keeping the Pentecostal movement within the church rather than creating a new one, so far I have not been able to discover much evidence of the execution or praxis of the excellent principles Ranaghan enunciated. As mentioned above, his own community, the People of Praise, does not permit those who do not accept the teaching of the Pentecostal leaders to attend the open (noncovenant) meeting. Nor has the community found room for professionally trained people or priests on their teaching team. This accords little with Ranaghan's words ". . . we can accept all Christians as fully our brothers and sisters with all the possibilities for holiness."

It is also to be noted that Paul DeCelles took exception to Father Harold Cohen's public declaration of devotion and obedience to the Catholic church and her hierarchy at the International Conference held at Notre Dame in 1973. Father Cohen is one of the coordinators of the Loyola University, New Orleans, group and has a seat on the Service Committee. In an article in the July 1973 *New Covenant*, DeCelles stated, "I take issue with the notion that we should automatically obey a bishop who asks us to stop participation in the Catholic charismatic renewal." DeCelles is a married, permanent deacon.

Further cause for thought arises from the formation of meetings for men shepherds. These shepherds are drawn from different denominations, but it is especially noteworthy that two non-Catholic exorcists are prominent in these groups. In Chicago, one is purported to have cast out the spirit of Catholicism from a nun. It would seem that the leaders are looking for guidance from outside the Catholic church. For instance, it does not appear that any priest was either on the committee of five or the pool of eleven speakers and prayer leaders for the shepherd's meeting.[13] This might suggest that religious indifference is creeping in.

The Covenant

For the Radical Reformers the preaching of the gospel became an open invitation, not only to a new life with God and to a community of believers, but to a new covenant. As Franklin Littell states in *The Anabaptist View of the Church*, through baptism "the believer came under the discipline of a Biblical people" (to p. 85). A long training was required for membership in the early church, and similarly the Anabaptists did not add members readily to their community. The individual accepted baptism and placed himself under admonition by the brethren, for membership was based on the true conversion and commitment to a disciplined life. The people of the covenant became people who were known, who were "visible to themselves and to the world governed by the Holy Spirit acting in their midst" (Littell, *The Origins of Sectarian Protestantism*, p. 37). The covenant was "the highest expression of religious voluntarism short of martyrdom itself; the balancing factor was the power of the community to forgive sins" (Littell, *The Anabaptist View of the Church*, p. 85). The commitment to the covenant was made public through the water bath and baptism. Melchior Hofmann,[14] one of the Radical Reformers, compared this to the covenant of marriage:

That is then such a true and certain covenant as takes place when a bride with complete, voluntary, and loving surrender and with a truly free, well-considered betrothal, yields herself in abandon and presents herself as a freewill offering to her lord and bridegroom (Williams, ed., *Spiritual and Anabaptist Writers*, p. 187).

Further it was emphasized that only the mature and rational who can learn and understand can enter the covenant. Only adults can participate in Life in the Spirit Seminars. The Salem covenant of 1629 read:

We covenant with the Lord and with one another; and do bynd ourselves in the presence of God, to walke together in all his waies, according as he is pleased to reveale himself unto us in his blessed word of truth (Littell, *The Free Church*, p. 41).

John Robinson (1579[?]–1625), writing in favor of separation and covenant, says:

. . . in what place soever . . . by reading, conference, or any means of publishing it, two or three faithful people do arise, separating themselves fro(m) the world into the fellowship of the gospell, and the covenant of Abraham, they are a Church truely gathered though never so weak, a house and temple of God rightly founded upon the doctrine of the Apostles (Littell, *The Free Church*, p. 41).

Similarly, as we have seen, Catholic Neo-Pentecostal groups and communities have established a regular initiation cathechumenate which culminates in prayers for the baptism of the Spirit usually accompanied by tongues. I have pointed out the emphasis placed upon glossolalia by Type I Catholic Pentecostals, and thus it is interesting to note that the same phenomenon occurred at the time of the Radical Reformation (see Williams, *The Radical Reformation*, pp. 133, 443, 830).

Apparently the seminars are the only way of gaining full participation in the Charismatic Renewal. The seminars are clearly designed to bring one into concrete communities (*Team Manual*, p. 17), the most vigorous and influential of which are covenantal.

The World

Catholics and Calvinists of the sixteenth century believed that the world could be redeemed. Lutherans and Anabaptists took a more pessimistic view. Yet while Luther thought the Christian should remain in and of the world and compromise with it to some extent, the Anabaptists would not permit any compromise. Therefore they sought to create a Christian social order within the brotherhood. This they saw as the realization of God's kingdom upon earth. It is important to understand that for the Anabaptist the "other kingdom" was not merely something transcendental that belonged to another aeon or was to be experienced only after death but a reality to be expected and experienced in this life, "even though in a sort of metahistorical situation" (Herschberger, ed., *Recovery of Anabaptist Vision*, p. 108). The citizen of this true kingdom separates himself from the world. He is highly suspicious of its values, including even that which is usually called "culture," and he is alive to the working of "destructive, non-divine forces in the background" (p. 111). The Radical Reformer was involved in a fight between the kingdom of light and the kingdom of darkness (pp. 111–12). Discipleship demanded the complete withdrawal from this passing order and meant "a new social order living eschatologically in accordance with the 'new age.' "[15]

The Pentecostal attitude toward the world is similar to that of the Anabaptist and is revealed very vividly in the Life in the Spirit Seminars, which emphasize evil spirits and the sharp division between light and darkness. Seminar 2 (*Team Manual*, pp. 103–11) is devoted to an exposition of all that is "seriously wrong with the world." The cause of this evil is seen to be something beyond the power of mankind, something bigger than man can handle on his own—Satan, sin, and the dominion of darkness (p. 103). The two kingdoms and one's choice between them is emphasized very strongly in this seminar. Although the entire October 1972 issue of the *New Covenant* was devoted to social action, Type I Neo-Pentecostalism eschews social concern and social action, and its attempts seem to turn into evangelization. At the People of Praise prayer meeting, South Bend, Indiana, one can be rebuked by the coordinators for offering a prayer that shows social concern because such a prayer is seen as an attack upon the group for not engaging in social action.[16]

Some readers have interpreted Ralph Martin to be denying

the brotherhood of mankind (Martin, *Unless the Lord Build the House*, pp. 30–31). Stephen Clark (Cassette 1103) states that there must be a real separation between Christians and the world, that there must be a change in social relationships, and that salvation involves this change in relationship. We experience only *partial salvation* if we are not separated from the world. For Clark, the world is a sinking ship, and the Lord has called us to be a body that might save it. By spiritual separation from the world we know our people. Therefore, Pentecostals form a closely knit brotherhood away from the world. Likewise, as Harold S. Bender expresses it:

For the Anabaptist, the church was neither an institution (Catholicism), nor the instrument of God for the proclamation of the divine Word (Lutheranism), nor a resource group for individual piety (Pietism). It was a brotherhood of love in which the fullness of the Christian life ideal is to be expected (Herschberger, ed., *The Recovery of the Anabaptist Vision*, p. 53).

The brother ideology follows directly from the kingdom theology, for this includes a social ethic, although not in the sense that we usually understand it. "All individualism and individualistic concern for personal salvation is ruled out. No one can enter the kingdom except together with his brother" (p. 113).

Similarly, Pentecostal seminars state that the candidate's decision "involves moving from one kingdom (and one social order) to another" (*Team Manual*, pp. 19, 108). Once Pentecostals are received within the community there seems to be a certain loss of concern for "outsiders."[17] Pentecostal communities address each member as "brother" or "sister," and the head is seen as a father figure (*Team Manual*, p. 170). Thus on the whole, Type I Catholic Neo-Pentecostalism is forming communities that are withdrawn from the world and similar to those of the Radical Reformers. Fichter (*The Catholic Cult of the Paraclete*, pp. 9–11) describes it as the establishment of a spiritual counterculture.

The Great Commission

In both movements every member is expected to evangelize. Among the Anabaptists the command to evangelize was binding on all believers (Herschberger, *Anabaptist Vision*, p. 161). This was carried out to such an extent that some Radical Reformers condemned the Anabaptists for irresponsibility with regard to their family and professions, which they had left to become itinerant missionaries (p. 161). As Herschberger maintains:

Most significant were their assumptions that a great Christian culture, after a thousand years of Christian teaching, needed to hear the Gospel and that the responsibility of witnessing was not the professional task of a particular class of Christians. According to the Anabaptists, the Great Commission followed baptism and, therefore, it became the task of every believer. This was a revolutionary idea which if practiced generally would soon change the face of Christendom (p. 138).

The Great Commission based on Mark 16 and Matthew 28 brought a tension between the Anabaptist community and society. The Great Commission also meant a disregard of territorial ecclesial limits.

After the baptism of the Spirit, Type I Pentecostalism also urges all members to witness to the new life they have experienced. They even evangelize Christians, for they argue that Roman Catholics, in particular, have been "sacramentalized" but not "evangelized."

The message of the most popular books (Sherrill, *They Speak with Other Tongues*; Carothers, *Prison to Praise*; Pulkingham, *Gathered for Power*) used by these groups is evangelization, mainly through testimonies concerning the blessings they have received. This is also the whole import of the seminars.

Evangelical Separation

Radical Reformer Dietrich Philips's fourth ordinance for the True Church (the third ordinance is footwashing, which has been introduced into some Pentecostal households) is evangelical separation, without which the congregation cannot be maintained. The unfruitful branches must be cut off. "If offending members are not cut off, the whole body must perish (Matt. 5:30, 18:7–9), that is, if open sinners, transgressors, and the disorderly are not excluded, the whole congregation must be defiled (1 Cor. 5:13, 1 Thess. 5:14) and if false brethren are retained, we become partakers of their sins. Of this we have many examples and evidence in the Scripture (II John 10f.)" (Phillips, in *Spiritual and Anabaptist Writers*, p. 246). In his book *The Radical Reformation*, George H. Williams comments with wry humor (pp. 485 ff.) that Anabaptism in the Netherlands and in lower Germany became Anabanism. In the February 1967 issue of *Concern*, Dr. John H. Yoder avers that among the Anabaptists the primary issue was not so much infant baptism versus believers' baptism but the importance of fraternal (and presumably sororal) correction according to the precepts of Matthew 18. In fact the "rule of Christ" with reference to Matthew 18 was a fixed phrase in their vocabulary by 1524, before the final conclusions were reached concerning adult baptism. Menno Simons saw the discipline of the ban as the chief means of securing fidelity to the bond or covenant of the baptismal vows among the brethren (Williams, *The Radical Reformation*, p. 396), and, whereas the ban (based on Mat. 18:15–18) was common to all Anabaptists, shunning (based on 1 Cor. 5:11) was characteristic of the Mennonites. Menno saw the ban and shunning as part of the Christian imperative to love. By this he meant the preservation of the purity of doctrine and fellowship (p. 396). The ban took over the function of the sacrament of penance that Menno had used as a priest and which he now believed he reinstated in apostolic form (p. 397). The ban was a natural consequence of the attempt to solidify the work done by religious revival. Unfortunately rigor and legalism are frequently consequent upon the awakening of the spiritual gifts, genuine though these may be.

The following features of Mennonite evangelical separation are of interest in view of the Neo-Pentecostals' stand. First, among the Anabaptists, fraternal admonition and the ban were used, not only in the face of genuine vice, namely, carnal sins, but also upon those who dissented from the tenets of the Reformers (Wenger, ed., *The Complete Works of Menno Simons*, pp. 968–69). Second, the scriptural texts upon which the reformers based their practice were Matthew 18:13–17; Romans 16:17; 1 Corinthians 5:10; 1 Thessalonians 1:4; 1 Timothy 3:1–7; Titus 3:10, and 2 John 10. Third, the ban was imposed either by the whole congregation or by the elders; the practice varied (Williams, *The Radical Reformation*, p. 396). Menno Simons exhorted the elders, teachers, ministers, and deacons to give careful instruction on the ban and not to use it recklessly or unwisely (Wenger, ed., *The Complete Works of Menno Simons*, p. 974). Ulrich Stadler, speaking about the Hutterite communism, describes deacons exercising the power to punish with severity all those who are disobedient and obstinate. Fourth, the manner of practicing the ban varied in strictness, and lengthy discussions ensued concerning the position of the spouses when one party was banned. Menno Simons felt that separation was necessary.[18] Discussion also took place concerning the extent to which brethren should have business transactions and commerce with the banned. Menno Simons decided that daily commerce should be avoided but that the brethren should always observe charity and mercy in the case of necessary service. The question also arose as to salutation, and again Menno Simons advocated mildness and respectfulness, the giving of the common greeting of "good morning" or "good day." However, the banned should not be received into one's house or greeted as a brother but only given the worldly greeting (Philips, in *Spiritual and Anabaptist Writers*, pp. 266–67). Fifth, the use of the ban was open to serious abuse and could be employed as a political weapon. To our contemporary Mennonite brethren, the historical records of these incidents are a source of embarrassment and disappointment. Among some of the Dutch Anabaptists there was harsh use of the ban, which was "the cause of lamentable quarrels and regrettable divisions" (*Mennonite Encyclopedia*, vol. 1, p. 221). German humanist Sebastian Franck (1499–1542) reports:

There is much banning in their churches, so that almost every church bans the other, and there is almost as much freedom of belief as in the papacy. Whoever does not say yes to everything, his ears has God stopped, and they begin mournfully to pray for him. If he does not turn about, they put him out (*Chronica*).

In certain groups discipline became very strict, and there were many detailed rules concerning conduct, wearing apparel, marriage, realtionship with the outside world, and so on. In fact, many Mennonite schisms arose precisely over matters of discipline (*Mennonite Encyclopedia*, vol. 2, p. 69). At times excommunication was applied to leaders or even to whole groups and was used as a threat to maintain control or used against personal enemies or for minor infringements of rules or personal interpretations of them (p. 278). In the course of numerous factional disputes and schisms among the Dutch Mennonites (1560–1650), excommunication (including mutual excommunication of entire groups) was resorted to more than once. A sensitive reconsideration of the whole concept of discipline is given in *Concern*, February 1967, which contains a number of essays on the topic. The main emphasis is on reconciliation.

Pentecostal Exclusion

In light of the incidents which have occurred in the history of the early Anabaptists, it may be of interest to the oral historian to watch the following directions within the Neo-Pentecostal movement in the Catholic church. First, fraternal admonition has been recognized as an integral part of community life and has been seen as a special responsibility of the coordinators:

From the beginning of our community there has developed among us, and especially among the leadership, the practice of fraternal direction and correction, carried out in the love of Jesus. We have found that the Lord often uses us to help each other and the whole community through mutual advice, frank discussion of problem areas, and on occasion admonition (*statement from the Notre Dame-South Bend Service Board concerning N. pp. 2–3*).

Second, this statement from the local community, which spoke of the exclusion of a member in terms of advising the member not to attend meetings (p. 4), was clarified and given national and international application in the *New Covenant* of July 1971:

. . . this situation as regards N . . . was only an instance of a larger pastoral problem facing all of us, about not only what to do with . . . N.N. but with others in communities across the country. After a time of prayer some very "hard" but relevant passages were shared with the group by those who either prayed for them or recalled them (Titus 3:8–11; Romans 16:17–20; 1 Corinthians 5:9–13). The passages and sharing after prayer brought home to everyone the need to begin to understand how to deal with those in our communities whom the Scriptures refer to as "false brethren" and "wolves in sheeps' clothing."

Further clarification of the Neo-Pentecostal position on exclusion is manifest in a circular from the two overall coordinators of one of the Type I communities to their brothers and sisters in Christ. The document bears no date and is addressed to "brothers and sisters in Christ." Judging from the order of events it must have been written about September 1971, that is, approximately three months after the statement in the *New Covenant*. The first question that concerned the overall co-ordinators was whether the "sinful actions" of those excluded should be revealed in public. This had already been done in two cases, one in which "the sinful actions" were declared by word of mouth to leaders all over the country. Another case had been discussed at length by the Service Committee for Catholic Charismatic Renewal together with the Advisory Committee (the first committee comprising seven members and the second comprising twenty-six members from all over the country) at the leaders' meeting on the Monday following the Fifth International Conference which began on June 18. The accused was refused admission to the discussion, and the whole case was heard without her being present to defend herself. The local committee did not meet with the accused until after the publication of the "sinful actions," namely, on July 8, 1971. Catholic priests attempted to counsel the coordinators on this serious issue.

The second question to which the coordinators addressed themselves was the reasons for exclusion. I quote verbatim from a circular signed by the two overall coordinators of the community:

Exclusion from our community should be done for three reasons: 1) a person can be excluded for openly advocating things which are incompatible with Christianity. Sometimes this may involve advocating things which would be acceptable in other Christian groups but which call into question teaching that is the basis of our life together, e.g., if a person should openly teach that tongues is not a gift of the Spirit or that the Lord does not speak in prophecy today. 2) A person can be excluded from the community for actions which are incompatible with a Christian life. Paul lists such actions in 1 Corinthians 9:9–13 [*sic*], 6:9–11 and there [*sic*] is a similar list in Rev 21:8. What is clear from these lists is that the actions which merit exclusion are extremely serious. 3) Finally, a person can be excluded for seriously violating the order of the community and refusing to accept correction.

To the scriptural texts already cited in the *New Covenant,* the coordinators added 1 Timothy 1:20 (a case of blasphemy) and Matthew 18:15–16. Thus, the Pentecostal community has used every text upon which the Anabaptists based their practice of the ban except 1 Thessalonians 5:14 and 2 John 10. According to this Pentecostal document, exclusion is the responsibility of the coordinators of the community. It is viewed as a case of judgment and is essentially a "disciplinary action." At least one of the coordinators involved must be an overall coordinator. The community as a whole seems to participate only as the coordinators explain to the community that an act of exclusion is being considered and ask their prayers. When the person is excluded, an announcement is made to the community "and the community should be asked for the appropriate support." The coordinators put some restraints on the publicity of the "sinful actions," but still do not recognize the importance of complete confidentiality.

Although the document certainly recognizes the necessity of attempting to explain to the person that he is not rejected if he is excluded, one regrets that the actions of the Pentecostal group are not consonant with this teaching. As far as I can gather, the purpose of notifying people over the country is to request that they shun the banned. In one case a married couple who gave hospitality to an excluded member was banned from the prayer meeting, and in the same case some members of the community not only declined to speak to the person concerned but also refused the kiss of peace at the parish Mass. Others, however, attempted to show extra kindness. In another case, even merchandise was withheld from the offender until the group learned that this was against the civil law. What is perhaps more serious is the fact that the accused had received the sacrament of penance and absolution was overlooked. Of the cases I know, it is doubtful whether any of the "offenders" had committed serious sin in the eyes of the Catholic church.

Indeed, the whole process of Pentecostal exclusion throws into high relief the wisdom, discretion, and clemency of the Catholic church in her practice of the sacrament of penance. Here the primary object is reconciliation; the penitent knows that he is accepted; confidentiality is insured and the church maintains discipline in the most humane way.

Conclusion

The thesis of this chapter may be summarized as follows. Type I Catholic Neo-Pentecostalism appears to have embraced in practice a modified form of the majority of the ordinances predicated of the True Church by Dietrich Philips (Philips, in *Spiritual and Anabaptist Writers*, pp. 240–55). Type I Pentecostals have gathered a pure community with "correct" ministers (first ordinance); they practice "baptism of the Spirit" which is parallel to "believers' baptism," and they hold love feasts of the *agape* (second ordinance), for example, in the People of Praise Community. Some perform the washing of feet (the third ordinance). They clearly implement the fourth ordinance, evangelical separation, and the fifth, love as admonition. They embrace the sixth by living a godly life and openly professing the truth of the gospel. It is very likely that they would fulfill the seventh (suffering and persecution) if called upon to do so, but the question has not arisen yet. Finally, they use the model of the Bruderhof as described in Zablocki's *The Joyful Community*, especially with regard to community of goods (which varies in degree in the different communities); marriage, which must be approved or arranged by the coordinators; the family, which is established on fundamentalist principles; the brotherhood; the "harnessing of joy"; the pattern of leadership; and the exclusion system. This means that they have not only approved but implemented many Hutterian principles of the sixteenth century and the twentieth. Our next task is to compare traditional Catholic spirituality and Type II Catholic Neo-Pentecostalism.

NOTES

1. See S. Clark's cassette, *The World and Christian Community*, in which he states that the world leads us into sinful conditions. It is under the influence of Satan. We have only partial salvation if we are not separated from the world; however, we must try to win it for Christ.

2. In his book *The Psychology of Speaking in Tongues*, John Kildahl states: "It was often difficult to distinguish whether glossolalists were talking about their leader or about Jesus. The leaders were regarded with a special quality of adoration, in such a way that it was difficult for an observer to know where the influence of the leader stopped and that of Jesus began. An intimate, prayerful address was used in approaching both Jesus and the tongue-leaders" (p. 44).

3. The *Team Manual*, pp. 105–11, suggests that evil in the world is caused, not only by human agency, but also by demonic forces.

4. These successes are portrayed very vividly by Ralph Martin, *Unless the Lord Build the House*.

5. Although the *Manual* does not advocate leaving the church, some families and individuals have done so.

6. One notes the use of the definite article. For Type I adherents, the Pentecostal movement seems to be *the* life of the Spirit, not *a* life in the Spirit. Rome appears to regard Pentecostalism as a spirituality and, therefore, not necessary for salvation.

7. For a more detailed discussion of Rothman's view of the church, see Frank J. Wray, "Bernard Rothmann's View of the Early Church" in *Reformation Studies*, edited by Franklin H. Littell.

8. On his cassette recording *Survey of the Catholic Charismatic*

Renewal, Ranaghan does not support his statement ". . . we can accept all Christians as fully our brothers and sisters with all the possibilities for holiness."

9. In *The Anabaptist View of the Church* (p. 108), Franklin Littell states: "The Restitution which had occurred was full of meaning on the world map. The Anabaptists believed that they were forerunners of a time to come, in which the Lord would establish His people and His law throughout the earth." The Neo-Pentecostals express similar sentiments.

10. For the use of Rev. 21, see Dietrich Philips, "Twelve Notes on the Church," in *Spiritual and Anabaptist Writers*, pp. 255–60.

11. In "Twelve Notes on the Church," Dietrich Philips discusses the first ordinance of the church which states that she must have correct ministers, regularly called by the Lord. Philips refers to the Old Testament figures of Aaron and his children (pp. 240–41) as does Randall on his cassette *Growth and Decline in Prayer Groups*.

12. In "Twelve Notes on the Church," Dietrich Philips speaks of excommunication and says it demonstrates the highest love and the very best medicine for the offender's poor soul, as may be observed in the case of the Corinthian fornicator (1 Cor. 5:6).

13. See the announcement in the February 1975 issue of the *New Covenant* which publicized the Second National Men's Shepherds Conference, which brought together "5,000 leaders from Pentecostal, neo-Pentecostal and Catholic charismatic movements."

14. Of Type I it has been observed by a Canadian Pentecostal that "they lack a sensitivity to personhood." See also B. Zablocki, *The Joyful Community*, pp. 239–385.

15. J. Lawrence Burkholder in *The Recovery of the Anabaptist Vision*, p. 150. See also Franklin H. Littell, *The Free Church*, p. 70: "A Plain-spoken message about the sins of the world was proclaimed"; and George H. Williams, *The Radical Reformation*, p. 183, quoting article four of the Scheitheim Confession: "For truly all creatures are in but two classes, good and bad, believing and unbelieving, darkness and light, the world and those who are out of the world, God's temple and idols, Christ and Belial; and none can have part with the other."

16. Tape recording not in general circulation.

17. This term *outsider* is employed with regard to non-Pentecostals. "In the first seminar, we are dealing with 'outsiders'"

(*Team Manual*, p. 93). Fr. Joseph Fichter, speaking at the Charismatic Conference at Louisiana in 1974, commented upon the lack of social concern within the movement.

18. Menno Simons, "Instruction on Excommunication," section 4, "The true apostolic ban makes no exceptions" (Wenger, ed., *The Complete Works of Menno Simmons*, pp. 970–74).

5

Catholic Pentecostalism: Type II

In his speech at the International Charismatic Conference held at Notre Dame in 1973, Father Harold Cohen, S.J., remarked that, just as there were twenty thousand people gathered to celebrate the festival of the Holy Spirit, so there were twenty thousand ways in which the Spirit led each individual. This would appear to be the attitude of many Roman Catholic Neo-Pentecostal groups throughout the United States and also in Canada and overseas, where Pentecostalism has been adapted and integrated with local situations, adding a spark of fire and a new spiritual vigor to the community.[1]

I describe Type II Pentecostalism from my associations with Benet Lake Benedictine Monastery, Wisconsin; Boston College, Boston; Catholic University of America, Washington, D.C.;[2] a Denver prayer group; Weston State College in Gunnison, Colorado; the Mayer group in Florida; Loyola University, New Orleans; Loyola University, Los Angeles;[3] New Melleray Abbey, Dubuque, Iowa; Pecos Benedictine Monastery, New Mexico; and a prayer group in St. Louis, Missouri. This is not a complete list of places where one can find Type II Pentecostalism but rather examples known to me. I use material gathered from my visits, the writings of the groups, and tape recordings. I also sent out a questionnaire in February 1972. Although this questionnaire is now out of date and many of the groups may have altered in significant ways, the expense of distributing another one has precluded me from gathering more recent information. Of the questionnaires sent, 290 reached their destinations, and 130 were completed and returned. Of the groups that replied, approximately 90 used the Ann Arbor catechumenate, but very few had adopted the paraecclesial structure. Only 10 had covenant agreements; only 19 had formal officers; and only 27 agreed to the use of the exclusion texts (particularly Matt. 18 and 1 Cor. 5). Many were deeply opposed to such a practice.

The groups showed quite a breadth of variety. In the "secular" (distinct from the "religious") groups, the number of members ranged from 3 to 500; 90 had under 100; 5 between 200 and 300; and 3 between 300 and 500. The percentage of Roman Catholics was interesting: 64 groups had over 90 percent; 29 groups between 70 and 90 percent; 16 between 40 and 65 percent; and 3 below 40 percent. The lowest was 5 percent.

The groups were predominantly white, 53 being all white; 43 being over 90 percent white; 3 over 60 percent; and 3 over 50 percent. One group was 70 percent American Indian, and one group 80 percent Chicano. The groups showed a greater sacramental and clerical involvment than Type I. Sixty-two combined liturgical functions with the prayer meeting. Many took an active part in non-Pentecostal parish activities and, as individuals, engaged in social action. From the questionnaire I could not discern any anti-intellectualism or anticlericalism; 27 persons (including women) showed an interest in training for the diaconate. Some received religious and priestly vocations. Many witnessed to a deeper love for the Eucharist and Mary than they had known before their Pentecostal experiences.

I should like to stress the amicable relationship between Type

II Pentecostalism and the Ann Arbor–South Bend type, and to observe that certain members of the former group are invited to speak at the international conferences. However, only two Type II members have seats on the Service Committee (1975).

General Characteristics[4]

Type II groups tend to be unstructured and free. For example, the Loyola University group (Los Angeles) drew over seven hundred people each Thursday in 1974, and, although the Life in the Spirit Seminars are used in modified form, there is no set format for the release of the Spirit. Each individual follows the Spirit as he leads in a unique way. Thus a priest or sister or lay person with spiritual experience would in no way be obliged to follow certain courses or seminars. There appears to be no covenant commitment, although there are households, and the groups do not look for leadership elsewhere than in their diocese among priests and mature lay men and women. The nominal leader at Loyola, Los Angeles, is a priest theologian who lectures on the charismatic movement on a university level.

From my questionnaire and from discussion with people attending the 1973 conference, I learned that, in contrast to the People of Praise community in South Bend and the Word of God, Ann Arbor, Michigan, which is at least 40 percent non-Roman Catholic, Type II groups are both clerically and sacramentally oriented. Some celebrate the Eucharist after their meeting or on days of recollection, and confessors are available for the sacrament of confession. Women are accepted as equals[5] and not kept separate, and they minister similarly to the men except for sacerdotal powers; some desire to become women deacons or even priests. At the Loyola University, Los Angeles, 1974 conference, there was a public penitential service with private reception of the sacrament of reconciliation for those who wished the "healing of the memories."[6] There was also discussion concerning a public unction for the sick for physical healing and spiritual strengthening of the infirm according to the new rite from Rome. These groups have wholly integrated the modern sacramental teaching and practice of the church in a most effective way. For them the church is their community and their covenant, and covenant renewal is found in the sacraments of baptism and the Eucharist.

In what was perhaps the most inspiring talk at the 1971 conference, Father John Quinn from Florida spoke on *The Spirit in The Sacraments* (Cassette 152). Referring to Matthew 18:20, Father Quinn emphasized that the phrase "when two or three are gathered together" refers primarily to the liturgy. He stressed the importance of keeping in contact with the church and affirmed the communal aspect of infant baptism and of seeing men and women as ecclesial beings. He suggested the renewal of baptismal vows during the Life in the Spirit Seminars and the use of holy water for deliverance from evil spirits. He suggested also that prayers for the baptism in the Spirit contain some reference to confirmation. He would like to see facilities for priests to administer the sacrament of confirmation so that more attention could be paid to the individual. He wished to see the introduction of Catholic liturgical thought into the prayer meetings and placed a value on liturgical life first, prayer meeting second. Throughout the talk he cited very good patristic sources. He emphasized that if the prayer meeting is not "plugged in" to the liturgy it will become dry bones.[7]

The groups under discussion here are not threatened by contemporary theology or academic pursuits and are taking a great interest in other Spirit-led movements such as the renewal of thirty-day retreats. The members relate easily with other Christians, non-Pentecostal and Pentecostal, Catholic and non-Catholic, and invite them to speak at their conferences; they also invite the Ann Arbor–South Bend members. Thus it would seem that this type of Catholic Neo-Pentecostalism fits more readily into the "mystic type" discussed by Troeltsch in his well-known study of the church, sect, and mystic types of religious life. The mystic type has deep religious experience but does not become legalized.

However, more importantly, the mystical tendencies in these groups are deepened by three significant features. First, the Benedictine and Dominican monasteries and other religious communities play an important and creative role and invite people to stay at the monasteries to build up a prayer life around the liturgy, the divine office, and the sacraments under the guidance of trained personnel. Indeed, some monasteries, such as Benet Lake, Wisconsin, see Pentecostals and other prayer movements as their new oblates. Second, instead of stressing the gift of tongues and attempting to make people yield to tongues, Type II Pentecostalism offers the liturgical office, the rosary, silence,[8] and above all, the Jesus Prayer ("Jesus, Son of the Living God, have mercy upon me a sinner"), as important aids to contemplation.[9] They also stress music and the creative arts, which have a humanizing and contemplative force, and intelligent use of Scripture. From the beginning these groups have welcomed both men and women trained in biblical studies. In the Ann Arbor–South Bend type, Scripture scholars were not invited to speak until the International Conference held at Notre Dame University in 1972, at least four years after the movement began.

Type II groups are also socially concerned and involved. To note but two examples; about eighty deaf people attend the charismatic meeting in Albuquerque, New Mexico. Deaf people do receive the gift of tongues. In Montreal, convicts from the local prison and alcoholics are invited to prayer meetings. They return to form prayer meetings in their own milieu. These Pentecostal groups are seen as a focus of healing. Exclusion, such as practiced in Ann Arbor and Notre Dame, is not used. Doorkeepers are not employed in these groups.

Most interesting, too, in Type II groups is their interest in the

Christian Orthodox church. Some groups seek to supplement their theology of the Spirit, and to adopt theological terms, from the Orthodox rather than from classical Pentecostalism in order to avoid confusion, for example, "baptism of the Spirit" with the sacrament of baptism. The art of prayer[10] as practiced by the Orthodox church is also taught through anthologies of Orthodox writings and lectures of guest speakers.

Type II Pentecostalism also encourages the talents of women and a devotion to Mary, both of which are essential to the mystic life because they bring with them a receptivity, a humanizing element, and sensitivity to the needs of others.

Remarks on Individual Groups of Type II

Our Lady of Guadalupe, Pecos, New Mexico

Perhaps the most important center for Type II Pentecostalism is the Benedictine Monastery of Our Lady of Guadalupe in Pecos, New Mexico. Thousands of people pay visits to this religious house, and all seem to be helped in a remarkable way. They are not asked to remain there permanently or to make a covenant. A few, but not many, may find a permanent vocation in the monastery, but this is not the main ministry of the monks and their sister helpers. Some people make short commitments. The atmosphere of this monastery, the daughter of the one at Benet Lake, Wisconsin, breathes freedom and joy.

Several monks went to New Mexico to found a new community. This is, of course, in the tradition of Benedictine monasticism which discourages large communities. However, both monasteries remain "mixed," that is, have Pentecostal and non-Pentecostal residents and activities. David Geraets was the first Catholic Pentecostal to be consecrated abbot. The transfer to New Mexico was not occasioned by friction or a wish for a separate type of spirituality. Benet Lake still continues to have a flourishing prayer group, and it is thought that participants are perhaps twentieth-century oblates, although they are not formally professed.

The monthly newsletter the *Pecos Benedictine* (hereafter referred to as *PB*), is a good source of information for the type of activities that engage the monks and those who assist them. It is not possible to survey all of these in a short work such as this, but I would like to highlight some of the important features that have appeared in issues from December 1973 to March 1975.

The monks work hand in hand with religious women and travel far and wide to give retreats, days of recollection, and Pentecostal conferences. They seem to be engaged in the widest possible areas of spirituality to help people of widely differing circumstances. At their own monastery they provide both ordinary retreats and Pentecostal retreats. One special feature is their family weekend retreats (see January 1974 *PB*) where they provide parents with babysitters and even play equipment. Their spirituality is extremely diverse, and they welcome all who love Jesus and even those who do not, that they may know him. They are deeply involved in houses of prayer (*PB*, December 1973) and thirty-day retreats (*PB*, November 1974). In their own monastery people can become novices (*PB*, October 1974), but others make a personal commitment for short periods, For example, three months (*PB*, July and October 1974). Their view of the individual approaches to prayer is expressed as follows:

The opportunities to pray with others during the day enrich our prayer. On Sunday, of course, we can join with our congregation in the more formal Mass or worship service. But explore the possibility of fitting a weekday Mass, an evening service, a home Mass, a visit to the Blessed Sacrament into your daily schedule. Such community worship in signs, symbols, and sacraments gives scope to aspects of prayer that might otherwise remain atrophied.

At home, learn how to seize the moments when the family can

experience its own uniqueness by praying together; meals, when one member is sick or troubled, little customs and ceremonies to bring out the significance of the feasts of the church year, Bible reading sharing sessions. Each family is different. Analyze the life style of your family to see what openings for group prayer either exist or can be created. . . . These are but a few of the myriad modes of prayer. For each person, learning how best to communicate with God is an adventure and a continuing revelation. The words of Alexis Carrel ring with enduring validity: "True prayer is a way of life; the truest life is literally a way of prayer" (PB, September 1974, p. 7).

The heart of this spirituality is the Catholic liturgy and sacraments and a nonfundamentalistic reading of Scripture. This does not mean that there is no ecumenical side. There is a book list in each issue of the PB, and from these items one sees the gentle blending of traditional spirituality,[11] for example, Carmelite, Franciscan, Dominican; Orthodox spirituality; Pentecostal and modern prayer methods, not even despising Zen (PB, June 1974). Pecos seems to have reached the right balance and to practice ecumenism but not religious indifference. Pecos has nourished vocations to the diaconate and to the priesthood (PB, March 1974). All the monks are well educated, some with doctorates, and there is evidence that they encourage the study of theology on an academic level (PB, June and October 1974). Abbot David and two sisters joined in the College Institute on Pentecostalism, which provided the first serious academic program for the study of the Pentecostal movement (PB, May 1974). Type I groups did not advertise this institute which was open to everyone. Several small theological conferences have taken place before in Dallas, Texas; Notre Dame, Indiana; and at the Bergamo Center, Dayton, Ohio; but these were restricted to scholars and theology students. Pecos is not reluctant to mention Catholic doctrine explicitly, such as the Eucharist, infant baptism, or Mariology (PB, December 1973). Abbot David, speaking of the immaculate conception of Mary's soul, says that its significance lies in the fact that God demonstrated that he was beginning a whole new order. He states, "We need Mary not only because Christ was formed in her physically, but because she shows us how we are formed to Christ's image" (*PB*, December 1973).

Pecos is deeply concerned on the social level and is involved in a multiplicity of projects: youth movements, work with retarded children, youth weekend movies, study, music, workshops on photography, candle making, art welding, chess tournaments, and so on. This is particularly the province of Brother Mark (*PB*, December 1973). Brother Gerard directs volunteers for PAL who go from the United States to Mexico to help with plumbing, electrical wiring, glazing, carpentry, painting, stonefence building, tree trimming, and gardening (*PB*, May 1974). Abbot David shared fellowship with twenty-five inmates of the state penitentiary on April 28, 1974. The monks have also sponsored the Hand of Help mission in Mexico. By July 1974, about eight hundred Mexican children were receiving help. Father Louis implements parish duties in Villanueva, an ancient New Mexican town where some families have lived for three hundred years (*PB*, January 1974). Even a sewing school for Mexican girls has been established. After a few months stay at the Hand of Help Center, a group of older girls set up a factory in their own village (*PB*, December 1974).

Thus Pecos seems to have attained Pentecostal poise. The first Southwest Charismatic Conference was held at Glorieta, New Mexico, in May 1975 (*PB*, January 1975).

The Southern California Renewal Communities

The Southern California Renewal Communities (SCRC) hold an annual conference. From this and their newsletter may be gauged the nature of their charismatic renewal. They declare the Life in the Spirit Seminars to be a "series of seven consecutive seminars, a step-by-step journey through the Gospel message, . . . more than informative, more than worthwhile but optional project for charismatic prayer groups" (*SCRC Newsletter*, 1973). When recording the goal of the seminars, they do not mention tongues, and they include the celebration of the Eucharist in the fifth seminar. They specifically include priests both in the Life in the Spirit Seminars and as spiritual directors. After the second Charismatic Conference they invited Father Hampsch to be their spiritual director. Instead of emphasizing tongues, they advocate the Jesus Prayer or the Rosary as repetitive heart (distinct from cerebral) prayer which can bring the same result as tongues.

The programs for the 1972 and 1973 conferences at Loyola University, Los Angeles, show a growing rather than a narrowing range of interests. Sessions concerning theology and pastoral vocations included approximately eleven talks by priests and panels of people from different denominations. A special talk on psychology was delivered by Dr. Morton Kelsey, Episcopal charismatic minister from Notre Dame, who has never been asked to speak at the Notre Dame Conference. Members of Type I Pentecostal communities were also asked to make contributions.

At the 1973 conference even wider interests were in evidence, demonstrating that all that is good and beautiful in the world was open to the movement of the Holy Spirit. The chairman was still a priest, and the conference included a communal sacramental penance service. There was also a prior suggestion that a public sacramental unction service be held, but this was not implemented last year. Other prayer and/or liturgical features were teaching on: the four "baptisms" of repentance, sacramental baptism, "baptism in the Spirit," and baptism of suffering; *lectio divina*, how to meditate on the Bible; the Jesus Prayer; the role of Mary;[12] meeting the Savior in the sacrament of penance; light in darkness, the classical doctrine of interior trials; the healing of the memories; discernment of spirits; and the Lord of the Dance, a symposium on dance as a means of liturgical prayer. The Eucharist was celebrated every day. The conference also showed an interest in arts other than dance by sponsoring an icon exhibition accompanied by a lecture. The comment under the description of the seminar read, "This consideration, far from being peripheral to the charismatic renewal, will be important in the development of the rich Christian spirituality into which we are being led." Drama was not omitted. Genesis, a gospel-rock chorus from St. Hedwig's parish, Los Alamitos, performed for the first time its new gospel-rock opera on the major incidents in the lives of the first Christians, entitled A Musical Pentecost! Further, under the title Creativity and the Holy Spirit, a team of artists led a seminar on the role of the Spirit in man's expressive faculties and the relationship of art to worship. One left the conference feeling that this is what charismatic renewal is all about. This Pentecostal Catholicism appears to have an exciting future. It is integrating the best of Western and Eastern spirituality and might well be a source of unity between Orthodox and Catholic communions.

This group of communities produces a newsletter, a mimeographed magazine Share, and tape recordings under the title Kerygma.

Lafayette Charismatic Conference

Another conference, different but equally good, was held at Lafayette, Louisiana, in November 1973. A conference was also held there in 1972, but I have no details concerning it. Diocesan conferences are now becoming quite popular and very successful. The November 1973 conference had a priest director who worked with a very representative group of men and women. At the International Conference held each year at Notre Dame

University, Indiana, on the other hand, only a chosen few (all white) are asked to speak at the assembly, and one is told to pray that the Spirit will say what he wishes through them. The arrangement for the Louisiana Conference was as follows:

We encourage you to be open and sensitive to the promptings of the Holy Spirit in this area. In order for everyone to be up-lifted and encouraged through the word gifts we ask that they be spoken loudly and clearly so that all may hear. The microphone on stage will be available and we encourage its use if needed. . . . We ask that you direct all announcements to the communication table near the stage (*Program for the Conference*).

The conference showed that the members of these groups were able to face problems and to reflect on criticism where necessary. Father Joseph H. Fichter, S.J., gave three addresses: "Charismatic Renewal and Social Action," an area he feels lacks emphasis; "The Role of Women in the Charismatic Renewal," a subject which is very controversial because of the subordination theory taught by Ann Arbor–South Bend groups; "Is Schism Latent in the Charismatic Renewal?" The comment after this heading read, "Does renewal cause division? Is it leading to a new Church? Burning issues, with a look at ideas on community. A sociological viewpoint, important considerations for leaders." Father Kilian McDonnell, a theologian studying the movement, presented an overview of the movement, "Catholic Charismatic Renewal-Reassessment and Critique." Two other subjects of great importance were also treated. "Finding the Lord's Freedom in Marriage" discussed *mutual* submission, an approach differing from Larry Christenson's book *The Christian Family*. The other subject was "Children and the Holy Spirit." Abbot David Geraets spoke of the transfiguration as part of the Christian life, emphasizing the Eucharist. There were many other excellent talks.

Type II includes Loyola University, New Orleans, which has been blessed by the presence of priests who have made a great contribution to the balanced growth of the movement. Some of these are: Father Harold Cohen, S.J.; Father Joseph Fichter, S.J.; Father Richard Chachere, diocesan representative for the Charismatic Renewal (Lafayette diocese); and Father Donald Gelpi, S.J., theologian, now in Berkeley, California. The presence of these scholars has helped the movement to remain healthy, to learn very quickly to accept academic dissent, and to face other difficulties. Father Gelpi has stressed the sacramental aspect of the movement and sketched the dangers inherent in similar historical movements. Father Cohen and Father Fichter have deepened the social concern of the members of the various groups. The intellectual level of the conference, as far as one can judge from the program, was high. (I was invited to the conferences but was unable to attend owing to teaching commitments at Notre Dame.)

The New Orleans pastoral team, which is composed of both men and women, made a presentation at the International Conference held at the University of Notre Dame in 1974. They provided the following guidelines (a mimeographed sheet given to the audience) for beginning a charismatic prayer group in a parish: (1) Place everything in the hands of God; (2) attend one of the larger prayer groups; (3) attend the Life in the Spirit Seminar and be prayed over "for a deeper life in the Holy Spirit" (this is careful wording which does not deny that other Christians have the Spirit or that the sacrament of baptism does not give the Spirit); (4) begin smaller prayer meetings as well as attending the larger ones. The fifth guideline is as follows:

You are probably ready to be recognized as a *parish* charismatic prayer group when the following situations have come about:
a) There are a dozen or more parishoners who have been meeting regularly to pray in the small group and they are mature enough in the charismatic gifts to sustain a *charismatic* prayer meeting at which other parisoners would be present.

b) There is real *leadership* to sustain such a charismatic prayer group. If you feel you must invite an outsider to come lead your prayer meetings, you are probably not ready to be recognized publicly as a *parish* charismatic prayer group. When the Lord wants you to be a *bona fide parish* charismatic prayer group, he will give you the leadership from within your own parish. Otherwise, it is like having an outsider come to your parish to "put on" prayer meetings.

If this leadership does not seem evident within your small group, just continue to meet in one another's homes, asking the Lord to raise up leaders among you. If a small group like this does not have leadership, it can hardly expect to exercise leadership when it begins to operate on a larger scale when other parishoners start to attend.

c Your pastor is willing to give you support, encouragement, and the use of a parish facility for your prayer meetings.

In observations on the guidelines, the group emphasizes patience, for the renewal will come in God's time. One should focus on Jesus, not on success.

Father Harold Cohen also distributed a mimeographed sheet entitled "A Vision of the Goals and Directions of the New Orleans Catholic Charismatic Community." This group began in 1969. There are now three weekly prayer meetings which draw a total of about one thousand people. In addition there are thirty-five other prayer groups in the metropolitan area. There is a pastoral team of five and an advisory council. From the fall of 1972 to the spring of 1973 they prayed, discussed, and examined closely the idea of a covenant group, but the Lord did not seem to be leading them in this direction. Thus they have remained a community without a covenant. Their community, therefore, "comprises all the people involved in the charismatic renewal in the New Orleans area in prayer groups that are predominantly Catholic." From my own observation it appears that this has prevented the development of elitism. The group appears very open, flexible, loving, and deeply socially concerned. The pastoral team has liaison with leaders of retreats, days of renewal, and other ministries. Its members are Father Cohen, head and Archbishop Hannan's representative, two laymen, one religious brother, and one religious sister. The advisory committee has nine members, and there is a full-time secretary. These people feel they are called to serve locally (thus differing from Type I people who apparently see themselves as international leaders). The smaller prayer groups foster life in the parishes. One group has introduced over thirty priests by inviting them to celebrate the Eucharist at their meeting. In addition to spiritual ministries, the community serves the poor and engages in ecumenical activities. It also hosts the Southern Regional Service Conference (in collaboration with Charismatic Renewal Services). It seems that this community is an excellent model for the Pentecostal movement to follow.

St. Louis, Missouri

Almost from the beginning of the Pentecostal renewal there has been a large meeting at the Visitation Academy, St. Louis, Missouri. It has always been sacramentally oriented although it is ecumenical. Religious sisters have played important leadership roles without hindrance from fundamentalist interpretation of Scripture. Many priests belong to the group. The one whom most people know is Father Francis MacNutt, O.P., but for some time now he has been away on journeys, especially to Latin America, conducting spiritual renewal with special emphasis on healing of body, mind, spirit, and personal relationships. He normally works with an ecumenical group of men and women. Frequently he has had the assistance of Mrs. Barbara Schlemon, a registered nurse and mother of five children, whose husband fully endorses her mission of healing. She resides in Florida and has always been a woman of deep prayer, even before the Pentecostal renewal. She attended the Benet Lake group but is not affiliated with any covenant group. Indeed, her work would be restricted if she were.

Father MacNutt has written an important book, *Healing,* which treats the subjects of the underlying meaning and importance of the healing ministry; faith, hope, and charity as they touch upon the healing ministry; four basic kinds of healing and how to pray for each; special considerations, for example, discerning the root of sickness, eleven reasons why people are not healed, the sacraments and healing, and answers to frequently asked questions. Father MacNutt has training in psychology in addition to his theological qualifications. He has sponsored a number of healing symposia to study the subject on a theological level. I have been present at two such meetings.

Since Father MacNutt has been called to a traveling ministry, a great deal of the responsibility for the Pentecostal renewal in St. Louis has been placed in the hands of sisters who are theologically trained. Two such are Sister Philip Marie and Sister Sharon Ann. They work closely with Cardinal Carberry and wait patiently as the Lord reveals their path step by step. In July 1973 the two sisters (members of the Sisters of the Adoration of the Most Precious Blood Congregations of O'Fallon, Missouri) asked for the blessing and encouragement of the cardinal as they seek to serve the church "by providing traditional Catholic teaching on the Charismatic Renewal in the Catholic Church. This teaching is based on a study and love of Sacred Scripture, the Sacraments—especially Baptism, Confirmation, Penance and the Holy Eucharist—liturgical and personal prayer, and the documents of Vatican II" (from photocopied circular). These sisters give modified Life in the Spirit Seminars that last eight weeks. Both sisters have postgraduate degrees, are experienced in retreat work, and were on the advisory board of Thomas Merton Foundation, St. Louis. The purpose of the Merton house was to deepen personal and community prayer life. They use as their main teaching tools: (1)

The Life in the Spirit Seminars Team Manual; (2) the Sacred Scripture; (3) the Vatican II documents on the sacraments, liturgy, the laity, and religious roles; (4) the lives of charismatic saints such as Our Blessed Mother, the Apostles, Sts. Dominic, Francis of Assisi, Benedict, Theresa, Teresa of Avila, John of the Cross, Catherine of Siena, Philip Neri, and Ignatius Loyola.

One can see how Catholic this is compared with the Life in the Spirit Seminars conducted by Type I Pentecostals. Using such teaching the sisters serve the parish school, both teachers and children; senior citizens; young mothers; separated and divorced people; married couples; college and teenage students; people attending charismatic retreats; and professional people. The sisters are anxious to avoid fundamentalist interpretation of Scripture, to enhance sacramental life, and to provide different prayer modes for the participants in their seminars, for example, the Eucharist (which is placed first on the list), praise, praying in tongues, repentance, the Jesus Prayer, prayer of silence, the Rosary, and litanies.

These are just a few of the flexible prayer groups found all over America and abroad. It would not be right to omit, however, a reference to people who went through the Pentecostal experience, gained much from it, and then launched into the mainstream of the church, committed wholeheartedly to her but uncommitted to specific prayer groups or communities, although they do attend meetings from time to time. Such, for example, are the first three people to experience the Pentecostal phenomenon at Duquesne University. One is a well-known church historian and liturgist, William Storey, who holds a university tenured position but also travels widely to lecture on the spiritual life, especially the divine office upon which he is doing work for the U.S. bishops. Among other works he has produced *Morning Praise and Evensong, Praise Him,* and *Bless the Lord.* He and Father Thomas McNally have prepared the *Notre Dame Prayer Book.* Another such Pentecostal, Ralph

Keifer, was editor of the *English Missal* and holds a teaching and liturgical position at an important seminary. He and I were co-authors of *We Are Easter People.*

In addition to literature emanating from academic circles, two important documents have been printed under episcopal auspices. The first is the Malines document entitled *Theological and Pastoral Orientations on the Catholic Charismatic Renewal* (Malines, Belgium, 1974). This is a good statement, but it does not address itself to some of the serious problems in American Pentecostalism. Indeed, sometimes it offers views opposed to the practice and teaching of Ann Arbor and South Bend, for example, on tongues, (pp. 51–52); exorcism, (p. 55); fundamentalist interpretation of Scripture (pp. 39–41); and the tightly organized *ecclesiola* (pp. 48–49). It does not deal with covenant communities.

The article "Charismatic Renewal, Pentecost Continues" in the May 1975 issue of *Origins* is a realistic appraisal of the movement by Canadian bishops. It describes both the merits of the movement and the dangers and is an excellent practical guide for Pentecostals.

I am hopeful that Pentecostal piety will continue to enrich the church, especially if it follows Type II Pentecostal Catholicism. As for Type I, its members are sincere and fully devoted to their Lord, Jesus Christ, and if they accept kindly criticism from outside their covenant communities, as they laud fraternal correction within, unity in the movement and with the church can be maintained. Although they are loyal to Jesus, he, the most intelligent rabbi who walked the face of our earth, seems to be urging them to listen to theologians, psychologists, and sociologists. The Spirit also seems to have a message for the American hierarchy of the Roman Catholic church and perhaps for other denominations. No longer can they stand as spectators of this powerful drama, which is moving swiftly across the ecclesial stage. They must become active participants.

NOTES

1. For example, in Britain there seems to be no trace of covenant communities or superstructure of any kind. These groups may be well represented by Father Simon Tugwell in his book *Did You Receive the Spirit?* This appears to be the best popular book on the subject of Neo-Pentecostalism on the market.

2. It would appear that the Pentecostal group which meets at Catholic University has quite a different ideology, sociology, and theology from another Washington group, Mother of God. The latter seems to fall into Type I and works closely with the Service Committee.

3. It seems that this group differs from the Neo-Pentecostal group in San Diego and from the community of John the Baptist, San Francisco. The latter two are influenced by South Bend and Ann Arbor, but this is not to say that their idea of community is exactly the same.

4. I do not wish to imply that none of these characteristics are found in Type I, but its extreme emphasis on community, on interpersonal relationships within the community, its uncompromising authority structure, and the close association with non-Catholic ministers rather than Catholic priests cause Type I to be theologically and sociologically unlike Type II in a number of crucial ways. In fact, it would be fair to say that the ideologies are quite distinct.

5. This is in contrast to the People of Praise Community, South Bend, which meets on Wednesday evenings and in which no priest or woman actively participates, either by leading meetings or by giving prepared talks at the open meeting.

6. Refer to Father M. Scanlon's cassette *Penance* or his pamphlet *The Power of Penance*. In Type I, more stress is given to physical healing and deliverance from demons.

7. For a total and exquisite integration of the charismatic movement within traditional Catholicism, refer to the excellent talk by Father D. Geraets on *Christian Community, Shared Prayer, Shared Living*, Cassette 137. Father Geraets stresses a discerning and revealing of the good qualities in people rather than the introspective approach of Stephen Clark on *Christian Personal Relationships*,

Cassette 120. For other talks which integrate the charismatic movement with traditional Catholicism, refer to Father Harold Cohen's *Priests and the Charismatic Renewal, the Priest's Full Life in the Spirit*, Cassette 132, and Father B. Songy's *Religious Communities and Charismatic Renewal*, Cassette 127. Father Songy advocates that a religious person should take full part in his or her own community even at the expense of the charismatic community. The talk is practical, sensitive, and deeply spiritual.

8. An excellent paper read by Dr. Richard Baer of Earlham College, Richmond, Indiana, is to be published by the Society for Pentecostal Studies. It points out the similarity between the prayer of the heart (distinct from the mind) which is practiced in liturgical worship, silence, and tongues; all have the same effect and are highly recommended. Information on the Society for Pentecostal Studies (a learned society) can be obtained from 1231 Olive Street, Eugene, Oregon 97401. The society members are scholars holding doctorates from various universities and are from all denominations but with an interest in the movement. At the 1974 meeting most speakers were black.

9. The Jesus Prayer was used by the early monks of the East. See Father David Geraets's book *Jesus Beads*, and Father George Maloney, S.J., *The Jesus Prayer*.

10. See *The Art of Prayer*, an orthodox anthology, compiled by Igumen Chariton of Valamo, translated by E. Kadloubovsky. Special teaching of Orthodox theology emanates from at least four places: Fordham University, where Father George Malone, S.J., is a professor of Eastern Christian Studies and active in the Neo-Pentecostal movement; the Benedictine monastery at Pecos, New Mexico, which distributes such texts as *Writings from the Philokalia on Prayer of the Heart* and *Early Fathers from the Philokalia*; and Loyola University, Los Angeles, through the studies pursued by Gabriel Meyer and others. From England comes Father Simon Tugwell's book *Did You Receive the Spirit?* which also gives much attention to the Eastern fathers.

11. In the May 1974 *Pecos Benedictine, Revelation of Divine Love of Julian of Norwich* is recommended. Morton T. Kelsey's *The Art of Christian Love* is recommended on the same page. Pecos invites writings and talks from three Notre Dame professors with whom the People of Praise, South Bend, do not have a relationship. Dr. Kelsey is an Episcopalian minister and professor at Notre Dame.

He specializes in religious experience and Jungian psychology. Pecos also promotes Ann Arbor and South Bend works.

12. See also *SCRC Newsletter*, vol. 1, no. 3, for a vivid witness from a priest concerning Mary's role. Cardinal Suenens also spoke on Mary at Notre Dame in 1974.

6

Affinities Between Traditional Spirituality and Type II

I believe that the Pentecostal movement, properly guided, can restore genuine mysticism to all Christian denominations. If I were to attempt to define *mysticism*, I should describe it as a life process or style in which the heart is kindled by an ardent love of God, the mind contemplates the supernatural in and above created things, and the will is set purposefully to the goal ahead. I speak here of heart, mind, and will to indicate that the whole person must be engaged in this enterprise. The mystic strives toward union with God in the dimension of the unseen and the absolute and, as he or she does so, becomes a more fully integrated human person. I am not concerned here with non-religious mysticism. Mysticism is not a moment or an experience or a psychic phenomenon or preternatural gifts, such as tongues, prophecy, or healing. Rather it is a lifetime growth in an interpersonal relationship with the trinitarian God and the surrounding world.[1] This growth will include conflict as well as "euphoria."

The pioneer of the mystic way is Jesus himself. One must note carefully, however, the way in which the Gospel material pictures him as such. The Gospels (and New Testament in general) do not present him *primarily* as a visionary. Only two or three visions are ascribed to Jesus: seeing Elijah and Moses during the transfiguration; Satan falling from the sky in Luke 10:18 (unless this is a metaphor); and the angel of the agony in Luke 22:43. Nor can he be seen as a tongue speaker since the only reference to Jesus' speaking in tongues is found in Irenaeus. Nor can he be viewed as a prophet in the strict sense, for if a prophet is one who brings forth the word of the Lord, can the Word of God himself be said to be a prophet?

Jesus does not belong to an elite community, such as the Essenes. His public charismatic ministry as exorcist, healer, and teacher apparently came after about thirty years of physical, mental, and spiritual growth. He repeatedly requested people not to publicize his miracles. The New Testament as a whole does not stress these ministries so much as his death, resurrection, and ascension. None of the Gospels draws a veil over his temptations, his rejections, his conflicts, or his mental and spiritual agony. The agony is given a fairly large amount of space in the Gospels compared to the description of the actual passion. Scholars have studied the affinity between the agony and the Our Father.

The Gospels allow Jesus' public ministry (prior to his resurrection) to end in miserable failure; seen from a worldly point of view, St. Paul would seem to have been a greater "success" than Jesus himself. The Book of Acts emphasizes that it was God (not Jesus himself) who raised Jesus from the dead, restored the glory which he had before. Only after this does he himself pour down his Spirit upon a group of fearful, trembling, but expectant men and women. Up to this point Jesus seems dependent upon the Father. In John's Gospel he is always dependent on him.

Thus Jesus' mysticism was characterized by "the naked intent of his will" and his total dependence upon the Father, his acceptance of the baptism(s) of suffering in his life through which he handsomely exhibited the fruits of the Spirit, and the strength of his inner self, in perfect freedom before the Father and mankind. His mystical union is expressed in his intimate relationship to the Father, shown in such texts as "I and the Father are one" and his use of "Abba" (Daddy). The best examples of Jesus' mystical prayer are found in the last discourses recorded in John 13–17. Mysticism in the church today must be viewed within this framework of the life, death, and resurrection of Jesus. There was no instant mysticism for Jesus; neither can there be for the twentieth-century Christian.

Having made these precautionary remarks, I turn to some characteristics of the mystic experience which are distinct from the mystic life as a whole (see Poulain, *The Graces of Interior Prayer*; James, *The Varieties of Religious Experience*, and Underhill, *The Mystics of the Church*). The heart of the mystic experience lies in the presence of God as felt or experienced. I quote one example: Ordinarily

God is hidden from him who has habitual grace and charity: he can neither have experimental knowledge of His *Presence* nor perceive it without a special favour. But by this union of fruition God manifests Himself to truly purified minds in such a manner that they perceive and taste *this presence directly and experimentally* by the knowledge and embrace of love. The real union of fruition of the contemplative soul with God is an *experimental and immediate* perception of God, produced in the intelligence and the will by the *real* presence of God. It is not the beatific vision; the mind, however, knows the divine presence, not only by faith, but through the gift of wisdom, by taste and experience (Poulain, *The Graces of Interior Prayer*, pp. 73–89).

This happens through the pure grace of God, independent of one's own will, although one may dispose oneself to this grace (Garrigou-Lagrange, *The Three States of the Interior Life*, pp. 409–27). The presence may be felt both "around" oneself as well as within oneself; sometimes the spiritual senses of hearing, touch, taste, smell, and sight are all present, but the most common is the sense of touch. However, both the mode of communication of the mystic experience and the knowledge of God gained from the experience are partially incomprehensible, obscure, and confused. Hence some Greek and Rhineland mystics speak of the "ray of darkness" or the knowing by not knowing (see McCann, ed., *The Cloud of Unknowing*). Union with God does not come about by reasonings or discursive meditation, but the ligature of the faculties *occurs*, that is, the mystic union *"impedes*, to a greater or lesser degree, the production of certain *interior acts* which could be produced at will in ordinary prayer" (Poulain, p. 178). Indeed, one might speak of being "struck dumb spiritually" when God gives the prayer of quiet or silence, the mere reposing in the divine presence without the noise of words or even interior reflections. The experiences of loving prayer are ordinarily interwoven with trials in the mystic life. These may be sickness, persecutions, interior sufferings, moral isolation, tedium or sadness (*acedia*), thirst for God, and distractions in prayer. The mystic does not pitch his tabernacle on cloud nine.

In light of the foregoing remarks, let us turn to Roman Catholic Neo-Pentecostalism. At first sight the conversions that take place, the exemplary lives of many members of the movement, the zeal for prayer, the thirst for Scripture, and the presence of the preternatural gifts, such as tongues, healing, prophecy, and miracle working, might invite one to identify this phenomenon with a mystical movement. However, one must not spring to an "instant conclusion." Three special cautions are necessary before we begin our investigation. First, if mysticism is a life process, then one cannot judge the movement within only one or even two generations. The formal movement, which began only seven years ago, has not been in existence long enough to allow a verdict. Second, mysticism is essentially an inward, individual experience. Therefore, it would be possible to notice nonmystics (and this is not to equate these with pseudo-mystics, i.e., charlatans) who have exterior gifts and to miss the true mystics who may be hidden by their seclusion or even by faults and trials which God permits. Third, Neo-Pentecostalism is one of the many prayer movements within the whole church today, and it would be necessary to compare it with some others. Many may be more "mystic" than Neo-Pentecostalism.

Bearing in mind these facts, however, one may investigate (a) whether there are mystic elements, but not necessarily mystical states, within the movement, and (b) how the Pentecostal movement prepares the ground for a mystic life.

With regard to the first point, common to nearly all facets of Pentecostalism is the baptism of the Spirit or the release of the Spirit. In my book *The Pentecostal Experience* and in articles in *Spiritual Life*, I have described the release of the Spirit as a touch of infused contemplation wherein there is an experiential sense of the presence of God and, I should add, an awakening to the power of the Spirit, especially for active ministries. Tongues and other accompaniments are not a necessary requisite for the "release," for essentially it is a "release" of love both for God *and* mankind. This release is followed by a variety of experiences. In one person it may lead to conversion from a very sinful life; in another to physical, mental, or spiritual healing; in a third, "conversion" from tepidity. In some it may be the beginning of a mystic life, but in very few, or none, I should dare to say, is it the seal of the perfection of spiritual life, that is, the state of union. I should surmise that the genuine central experience of Pentecostalism (and I have no reason to suspect that it is not so in most cases) is of a mystic nature, but it does not make "instant mystics." Moreover, this is not to deny that there may be other mystic elements, over and above the "release" in the phenomenon.

With regard to my second point of investigation, namely,

whether Pentecostalism prepares one for the mystic life, I believe that the Ann Arbor–South Bend type (Type I) is an evangelizing movement but does not appear to prepare the ground for mysticism. I see Type II Pentecostalism offering fertile ground for such. I surmise that in many ways Type II Neo-Pentecostalism will follow a development rather akin to the philosophy of the late Thomas Merton, founding itself deeply on the sacramental life, personal prayer, silent contemplation, and, in some cases, solitude. It can also branch out to touch all the social, political, and religious needs of the day as well as incorporating whatever might be Spirit-inspired in the non-Christian religions.

I see the principal source of, and the most appropriate place for, the "release" of the Spirit in the ecclesial community gathered for the celebration of the Eucharist, where the risen Lord will be present to bestow continually the gifts and fruits of the Spirit. I should define the "release of the Spirit" as an experiential or experimental sense of the presence of God of such strength that one knows with the deepest sense of certainty that one not only believes in God but *knows* him—in the Hebrew sense of the word[2] *know* as experience. In Catholic traditional spirituality this is known as the Presence of God Felt, and it is deemed to be a pure "gift" from God, a gift for which one can dispose oneself but that only God himself, as sovereign, can dispense. It is not acquired merely by human effort. I should like to cite two examples, one from a woman doctor of the church, Teresa of Avila, and one from a man. Teresa of Avila says:

I used to have at times, as I have said, though it used to pass quickly away,—certain *commencements* of that which I am now going to describe . . . and sometimes even when I was reading,—*a feeling of the presence of God* would come over me unexpectedly, so that I *could in no wise doubt, either that He was within me,* or that I was wholly absorbed in Him. It was not by way of vision: I believe it was what is called mystical theology" (Poulain, pp. x, 1).

Alphonsus Rodriquez describes the experience thus:

> . . . *This feeling of the presence of God* is not obtained by way of imagination; but it is in her (the soul) as a certitude received from on high: she has a *spiritual and experimental* certitude, that God is in the soul and in all places. This presence is called an *intellectual presence*. As a rule, it lasts a long time: the farther the soul advances in God's service, the more *continuous* is it, and the more *felt*. . . . without his even thinking of it, this sovereign Master has placed Himself sensibly before him, as a man should place himself suddenly before another, without this latter being aware of it, etc. (Vie de St. Alphonse, from his *Memoires*, No. 40, as quoted by Poulain, pp. 73, 76–77).

The experience does not mean that one is in a state of special holiness (i.e., a contemplative state), but it does mean that the Holy Spirit has invited one to commit oneself to a special pursuit of holiness (see Hilton, *The Ladder of Perfection*). In my opinion, the "release" is not a once in a lifetime occurrence— although the first experience is perhaps naturally the most memorable. If the Christian walks in the footsteps of Jesus, this "release" recurs, not only in the same modality, but in a varying number of modalities, not only throughout his or her life, but also in the afterlife. Hence the "release" is the first fruits of what we will enjoy in heaven, and the fullness of the Spirit will occur only in heaven.

In summation, I should say that I see the "release" of the Spirit as a series of experiences of God which are more vivid and real than most human experiences. But I see them also intimately and mysteriously interwoven with the theology of the cross. If the "release" (or awakening) is a "peak experience," then the cross is a "pit" experience; they go hand in hand (Geraets, *Baptism of Suffering*). This is wholly biblical. Our spiritual development is a sillouette of the life of Christ. Our sacrament of baptism may be compared to the descent of the Holy Spirit upon Mary at the annunciation. The Spirit is present, but there may be no outward or dramatic manifestation, or the manifestation may be so refined that the human mind or eye cannot discern it (1 Cor. 2:14–16); our sacrament of confirmation is akin to Jesus' Bar Mitzvah (Luke 2:41–52); our "release" should not be too closely associated with the sacrament of baptism or confirmation. It is more akin to Jesus' baptism, when we too are called to public witness. It may be followed by a temptation in the desert. Our further "releases" may be compared to the glorification on Mt. Tabor (or Hermon); this event was preceded and proceeded by the first two predictions, not only of Jesus' own sufferings, but also of those who should take up their cross and follow him (Mark 8:27; 9:50 and parallels).[3]

As we progress in the spiritual life, we become more acutely aware and more responsive to what I would name the "Roman," "Ephesian," and "pastoral Epistles" ministries. For this purpose in my book *The Ministries* I have drawn up a preliminary chart of ministries from 1 Thessalonians, Corinthians, Romans, Ephesians, 1 Peter, and so on. I differentiate between (1) evangelizing ministries; (2) solidifying ministries; and (3) pilot and discerning ministries. I conclude that, although all ministries are to be found within the church as a whole (and I speak of all denominations) and, while the Pentecostal spirituality presents one important and genuine group of ministries, the other ministries are found in considerable profusion in other parts of the church. My eyes had been partly closed to this in the early days of the Pentecostal movement. All these ministries must join together as the one body. Tentatively I have distinguished (but not made a trichotomy between) (1) "evangelizing ministries," for example, evangelists, miracle workers, healing, tongues, and interpretation; (2) "solidifying ministries," for example, teachers, prophets, one who exhorts, one who shares, one who does acts of mercy; and (3) "pilot ministries," for example, apostles, bishop, presbyter (pilot or administrator in 1 Cor. 12:28), deacon, deaconess, and widow. The "solidifying ministries" are often found among those dedicated and prayerful Christians, such as counselors, psychologists, sociologists, and teachers, who combine professional training with a deep spirituality (see Henri Nouwen's *Intimacy* and *The Wounded Healer*, Elizabeth Kübler Ross's *On Death and Dying*, and Simone de Beauvoir's *The Coming of Age*). But all these people must be fully committed Christians who have experienced the Lord Jesus. I have come to this view of the ministries through a consideration of the fruits of the Spirit (see Gal. 5:22 ff.) developed to a very high degree in my Christian friends—men and women—who practice the behavioral sciences for the benefit of the community. Indeed, I concur with a quotation from Dr. Smiley Blanton, director of the American Foundation of Religion and Psychiatry. When he was asked whether he read the Bible, he replied:

I not only read it, I study it. It's the greatest textbook on human behavior ever put together. If people would just absorb its message, a lot of us psychiatrists could close our offices and go fishing (Hembree, *The Fruits of the Spirit*, p. 45).

He went on to comment on how foolish it is not to make use of the distilled wisdom of three thousand years.

In a similar way it has become increasingly clear to me that the churches are wise to have not only an "enthusiastic" ministry but also a trained and appointed structural ministry. It would seem that we can trace the gradual evolution of a structural ministry *side by side with and not in place of* the enthusiastic ministry. My own thesis suggests that the permanent ministries such as bishop/presbyter (perhaps = *kubernēseis* of 1 Cor. 12:28) arose in the pastoral Epistles and the primacy text (Matt. 16 and 18) in response, not to Gnosticism or any other heresy, but to "over-enthusiasts" (*New Testament Studies*, 17:338–346). I would not, however, have seen this unless I had experienced both the beauty and power of the ministries listed in 1 Corinthians and also the dangers, such as divisions and rivalry among leaders found also in 1 and 2 Corinthians. The trained structural ministry serves as an anchor, or rather *rudder,* for the enthusiastic.

Indeed, Type II (and in some respects Type I) have implemented the above. However, one should add, too, that they have embraced some of the traditional theology, most especially that of the Benedictine,[4] Carmelite, Dominican, and Franciscan.

Franciscan Theology

Franciscan theology is primarily affective (involving the emotions) and must be distinguished from speculative and university-oriented spirituality, although the fusion of heart with mind is found especially in St. Bonaventure. Like the Franciscan order the Pentecostal movement in America finds itself in a country of wealth with a comparatively rich church. Both Type I and Type II endeavor to return to a simpler life more in keeping with the Gospel tradition, although Type I groups sell books and tape recordings. Unlike earlier religious congregations the Franciscans saw that their main duties were to evangelize and preach. This has also been true of both Type I and Type II Neo-Pentecostalism, but Type I is more inclined to bring a person into the prayer meeting than to go out and preach in the outside community.[5] Music, especially religious songs, is a characteristic of both types, but the songs of Type I appear to be more stereotyped than those of Type II. For example, a member of Type II might receive a song through the gift of the Spirit and teach it to the community. This does happen occasionally in Type I, but the groups of Type I are influenced so heavily by the prayer meeting leader, who is usually the same man each time, that there is less spontaneity.

Francis was frightened by the large numbers of people who

followed him. There seems to be a similar fear in Type II communities since large meetings seem naturally to break into smaller groups. The smaller the group, the less organization is necessary. Francis tried to make peace between the Guelphs and the Ghibellines, between the party of the pope and the party of the emperor. In a similar way Type II has tried to make peace between black and white, rich and poor (especially in Latin America), and it succeeds in being very sensitive to the discrimination with which women are treated both in the church and in Type I. Type II shows a deep love of the crucified one and values the sufferings of the cross (see Geraets, *Baptism of Suffering*) and is also ready to reap the fruits of creative conflict. As we have explained above, Type I tries to harness joy (see the discussion of the harnessing of joy in Zablocki, *The Joyful Community*, pp. 164–92) and maintain order and euphoria; negative feelings must be hidden[6] or exorcised. Like St. Francis, Type II develops a tender love of the name of Jesus, especially through the Jesus Prayer. Thomas of Celano said of Francis:

How many times when he was sitting at table and heard the name of Jesus spoken or pronounced, or simply called it to mind, would he not forget to take his meal? He was like the holy one of whom it is said that *seeing he saw not and hearing he heard not*. Even more, very often, when he was on the road and thought of Jesus and sang in his honour, he would forget his way and invite all created beings to praise Jesus.

Type I Pentecostals do sing hymns to the name of Jesus, but tongues takes precedent over the Jesus Prayer. The fatherhood of God reflected in all creation was a source of wonder and praise to Francis. In the same way Type II seems to have a devotion to the whole Trinity and to both the humanity and the divinity of Jesus rather than devotion to the Holy Spirit, and almost exclusively to the miracle-working and resurrected Christ. St. Bonaventure, a follower of Francis' teaching, developed the theory of the three ways of the spiritual life: the purificatory, the illuminative, and the unitive. These are also stressed by Type II, but Type I dwells much more on the illuminative and seems to fear slipping into a different state. In fact Type I Pentecostals understand dryness in prayer as indicating possession by a demon and even ask their friends or priests to exorcise them when dryness in prayer appears.

Type II has a much greater veneration for Mary than Type I, and this may be due to the greater catholicity or to its interest in the Orthodox church. This might be compared to the development of the passion of Mary among the Franciscans (Pourratt, *Christian Spirituality*, p. 187). The latter excelled in the dramatic medium when they evangelized the people (p. 188). This is of interest in light of the drama, rock music, and artistic talent developed in Type II. Further, the Franciscans developed the art of dying (p. 191). Type II has shown interest in the research on dying done by Dr. Elisabeth Kübler Ross and others. Finally, Sisters Philip and Sharon of Type II (Missouri) recently forwarded to me literature on Angela of Foligno, the Franciscan. The latter can be used as a model for some Pentecostals. Type I rarely refers to the saints and prefers following the example of contemporary fundamentalist ministry.

Dominican Spirituality

The Dominicans were very much involved in intellectual pursuits, and, in light of this, it is interesting to note that most of the more scholarly books by Pentecostals are written by members of Type II, many of whom are Dominicans or Jesuits. The Dominican Sisters have also fostered the study of theology, especially at the Theology Institutes, Siena Heights, Adrian, Michigan, which were combined with liturgical activities and prayer meetings. In my book *The Pentecostal Experience,* I pointed out the affinities between the ministries of the Spirit that are appearing today and the life and ministry of St. Catherine of Siena, doctor of the church. The Dominicans produced St. Thomas Aquinas, and it is pertinent to note that Father Edward D. O'Connor, one of the founders of the movement at Notre Dame, both teaches and writes on Thomas. The Dominicans, like Father Martin Hopkins, O.P., who organized a theological conference on the Pentecostal movement at St. Albert Priory, Irving, Texas, in 1971, also use Thomist theology in teaching Pentecostals. It is noticeable that members of Type I who live very close to the University of Notre Dame usually do not attend theological lectures or symposia at the university. Members of Type II engage actively in their theological professions. Type II's interest in art, and especially icons and religious art, may be compared to the Dominican artists, especially Father Giovanni Angelico of Fiesole (Pourratt, (p. 203). Women who belong to Type II are emancipated but not aggressive. Many of them feel called to the diaconate or to the priesthood and are pursuing avenues in this direction. One imagines that Catherine of Siena would have been among them had she been born in the twentieth century.

Carmelite Theology

Although Type I groups sell the works of Teresa of Avila and John of the Cross, there is very little evidence that these two are given much prominence if one compares the programs for conferences organized by Type I and Type II. The latter gives attention to the teaching of both saints and encourages the reading of their works.[7] Teresian spirituality is taught even to non-Roman Catholics and has been a most exciting and consoling revelation to them, for instance, at the Mennonite

Festival of the Holy Spirit held in 1973 at Goshen College, Indiana. The Pentecostal experience may be a touch of the state of illumination, but one cannot expect never to return to the state of purgation, which lasted nearly thirty years for Teresa (O'Connor, *New Catholic World*, November/December 1974). Further, Teresa's most active career was executed during her illuminative or unitive state, a fact that makes one realize that social and/or religious concern and action are neatly wedded to the most advanced stages of prayer. The same may be said of St. Catherine of Siena.

Another Teresian feature is her whimsical sense of humor (Peers, *Studies in the Spanish Mystics*, p. 120). Type I Pentecostals tend to be serious to the point of severity. This was not so at the beginning of the Pentecostal movement. It is useful to remind ourselves of Teresa's four stages in prayer. In the beginning one (1) labors strenuously for water (Teresa uses the metaphor of the water wheel) but has no mystical experience, one is distracted in prayer, and finds little recompense (Peers, p. 123). (2) In the prayer of quiet the contemplative soul need not toil for every grace. This stage lasts only for a very short time, indeed, sometimes it is only a little spark (pp. 124–125). Here the

important thing is that the soul should not seek to increase this fire, which—if it does so—it can only quench, by striving with the understanding—a temptation specially common among the acute-minded and learned. Let learning be put on one side—the time may come when God will use it, but for the present the contemplative should remain for as long as he may in the state of Quiet and wait upon the Lord (p. 125).

(3) In the third stage the Lord himself does the work, and the soul can reap spiritual sustenance without any effort; the virtues are stronger and sweeter (pp. 125–26). This also increases the humility of the soul. In this state the faculties (memory, understanding, and will) arc asleep. Often here

the subject speaks, perhaps—but without order or method, and the speech is all of God: the understanding counts for nothing here. So all that is heard is "a thousand holy follies" (p. 126).

This may be the gift of tongues, but Teresa does not use those words. (4) The soul is receptive and passive, for the grace of God is showered on soul and body in the fourth state. There is only rejoicing, for the will is occupied with loving, and the other faculties are suspended (pp. 128–29). This experience of union is usually only transitory.

Teachings such as these together with those of John of the Cross are enriching the Pentecostal movement. Type II is also deeply imbued with the theology of the Spirit, which is found in the Eastern Orthodox church and in Mariology.

Thus I should say that the Christian denominations, and most especially the historical churches, should not fear the Neo-Pentecostal movement but rather welcome it into their midst. On the other hand, Pentecostals must be ready to discern the facilitating or guiding power or grace of legitimately ordained ministers of the church. They must also embrace the theology of the cross and recognize that every spiritual gift is free from God and may neither be demanded nor acquired by purely human effort. I pray God to bless this movement and all other movements of the Holy Spirit in the world today, and I respectfully ask that we may engraft two slogans on our hearts: "Let us fly united but not in too close formation"; "The gifts may divide, the fruits *always* unite."

Notes

1. Mystics are often interested in nature and in intellectual pursuits, tendencies well illustrated in the Spanish mystics discussed by E. Allison Peers in his book *Studies in the Spanish Mystics*. They also tend to be socially concerned, e.g., Catherine of Siena.

2. I think that my definition would be consonant, but not identi-

cal, with E. D. O'Connor (*The Pentecostal Movement in the Catholic Church*); Simon Tugwell (*Did You Receive the Spirit?*); and Dr. Susan Anthony in her beautiful essay in *As the Spirit Leads Us*, edited by Dorothy and Kevin Ranaghan.

3. In his essay "Baptized in Water and in Spirit" in the book *The Baptism of the Holy Spirit*, Dr. Arnold Bittlinger has come to the same conclusion as the Roman Catholics concerning the three stages in an average spiritual life.

4. Benedictine spirituality is found in the groups which associate with such monasteries. However, it is very revealing to peruse some of the Pentecostal covenants, e.g., that of the former True House (which amalgamated with the People of Praise in late 1974 or early 1975). The covenants, in contrast to the Benedictine Rule, are essentially horizontal, that is, bonded through the brotherhood; the Benedictine Rule is vertical, that is, essentially Godward. The Prologue of the Rule is scriptural meditation. The True House covenant compares itself to the politico-legal system in the United States.

5. Larry Christenson, author of *A Charismatic Approach to Social Action*, appears to think that the Christian church should only concern herself in this way by bringing people into her community. He surmises that it is wrong for people to pay taxes to help the needy if this is against their will. See especially pp. 70–76 and 86–87 of his book.

6. In her article in the November/December 1974 issue of the *New Catholic World*, "Ignatius House: An Experiment in Pentecostal Community," Terry Malone says: "When disagreement is the issue, restrictions are even stronger. Members are asked not to discuss their negative feelings with one another, but to bring them to the shepherds. The reason given for this is that negativism is destructive to the unity which is seen as essential if the community is to survive. Therefore, whatever promotes unity is acceptable, whatever rocks it is not." I would substitute the word *uniformity* for *unity*.

7. For much of the following material I am indebted to E. Allison Peers, *Studies of the Spanish Mystics*, vol. 1.

7

Pentecostal Poise

This chapter will outline some strategies for keeping the Pentecostal movement charismatic, flexible, and well within the bounds of the Catholic church.

Reflections on the Life in the Spirit Seminars

I have described the Pentecostal catechumenate, which is the Life in the Spirit Seminars of Type I. The Seminars comprise seven classes in basic Christian thought and are designed (1) to bring the candidate on the fifth week to the experience of the "baptism" (or release) of the Spirit and speaking in tongues (*Team Manual*, p. 160) and (2) to initiate the candidate into a Pentecostal prayer group or a covenant community on the principle that this is not an optional choice because "normal Church life is not enough" (pp. 160–2). The seminars are used all over the United States and Canada and abroad, and the *Team Manual* is translated into a number of foreign languages. Already sixty-five thousand copies of the seminar manual have been sold. In view of the extremely widespread use of this manual, I wish to offer some reflections on it, and I hope that others, especially in the field of psychology and sociology, will also give the seminars some consideration. (For an accurate assessment of the seminars, it is necessary to consult the latest edition of the *Team Manual*.) I regret that it is necessary to begin with a negative approach, but the survey ends with some concrete and positive suggestions, especially about Scripture, the sacraments, and the official hierarchy of the church. In addition, it should be noted that many persons who use the *Team Manual* adapt it according to the needs of their situation.

Religious Indifference

One question that concerned the U.S. Catholic bishops in 1972 was a religious indifference that might emanate from the Pentecostal movement. This fear was expressed in their official statement (*Origins*, June 1972). The Holy Father expressed similar sentiments when he said:

Spiritual life consists above all in the exercise of the virtues of faith, hope and charity. It finds its foundation in the profession of faith. The latter has been entrusted to the pastors of the Church to keep it intact and help it to develop in all the activities of the Christian community. The spiritual lives of the faithful, therefore, come under the active pastoral responsibility of each bishop in his own diocese. It is particularly opportune to recall this in the presence of these ferments of renewal which arouse so many hopes (October 1974).

The *Team Manual* is professedly religiously indifferent. As the author explains it is designed to be "universal" and to present the basic message of Christianity "in such way that it could be received by every type of Christian" (*Team Manual*, p. 7). The seminars were developed in a community that is now at least 45 percent non-Roman Catholic. Robert Johnson (*Varieties of Campus Ministries*, p. 4) remarks that over forty denominations are represented at Ann Arbor. As I have mentioned earlier, the *Manual* stresses that one should by-pass all dogmatic or theological questions and go straight to people's hearts and recommends that serious theological questions be discussed outside the seminars. In practice this may mean that very often they are never discussed at all. The *Manual* also states that the speaker should avoid arguments and controversies in his talk, but frequently people report that they are disappointed because they are not permitted to question the statements of the seminar teacher. The teaching is authoritative and permits only the most controlled discussion. It is also averred that criticism should be reserved for "sin and inadequate ideas" (*Team Manual*, p. 41). There is a danger here of overlooking the intellect entirely; the mind as well as the heart is a gift from God. In his book *The Catholic Cult of the Paraclete*, Father Joseph Fichter notes that, for the average Pentecostal, "heart" often overrules "head." It seems that there should be room for intellectual discussion and academic dissent. Certainly the Gospels show that Jesus permitted it.

Moreover, it is stated that the seminars are for everyone, non-Christians, Christians, and those who are already baptized in the Spirit (*Team Manual*, p. 86). It would seem that one cannot cater to all these people through one set of seminars, and the risk is run of misinterpreting the scriptural texts. For example, how can one present texts concerning sacramental baptism in their proper sense to the non-Christian while at the same time presenting these texts in the sense of "release in the Spirit" to the Christian and to the one baptized in the Spirit? It is not quite clear why one who is baptized in the Spirit should go through these seminars, but perhaps it is in order to implement the proviso that all who want to be part of a covenant community or who want to teach the seminars must first have completed them (p. 41).

Important, too, is the stipulation that a team member must accept the *whole* message of the seminars before he or she is allowed to teach (p. 24). It is not said that he must accept the teaching of the church or of the New Testament but simply the seminars. This is crucial, since it discourages scholars who cannot accept the fundamentalist interpretation of Scripture found in the seminars from becoming members of the teaching team. To my knowledge no priest or scholar assists with the catechumenate at Ann Arbor or South Bend. The primary theologian has officially withdrawn from any leadership position in South Bend and does not attend the DeCelles-Ranaghan prayer meeting on Wednesdays at Christ the King. This should, indeed, be cause for the leaders to review their theological position and for the bishop to intervene.[1]

The complication of teaching non-Christians, lapsed Christians, Christians, and those baptized in the Spirit in the same course presents another difficulty. The *Team Manual* speaks about allowing people to see the salvation offered to them and their moving from the kingdom of darkness to the kingdom of light. But if they are already Christians, they are seeking increase in *sanctification*, not *salvation*, which has already been offered to them in the sacrament of baptism. All those in the state of grace are already in the kingdom of light. Very curious, too, is the *Team Manual's* apparent assertion that sacramental baptism is not always necessary:

We do not want to tell people that they *must* be baptized sacramentally in order to be baptized in the Spirit. Cornelius was not (Acts 10), and many people today are not. All that we should do is to make clear that sacramental baptism is important, and then use our discernment to advise individuals about the way to proceed in their own situation (p. 141).

It is strange that the *Manual* takes no notice of the New Testament or church teaching on this question. It would appear—but it is not quite clear—that the *Manual* considers "baptism of the Spirit" a substitute for sacramental baptism. The Cornelius case is cited without any reference to the fact that

Cornelius and his companions did receive sacramental baptism after the outpouring of the Spirit. In any case, Acts 9–10 is the exception which proves the rule, not the rule. Further, it is even more curious that McDonnell, writing on Christian initiation and the Pentecostal movement (*The Holy Spirit and Power*, pp. 57–85), does not refer to the *Team Manual* or any materials used in the Pentecostal catechumenate.

Group Dynamics Rather Than the Free Working of the Spirit

I have argued that the Seminars appear to be based on group dynamics rather than being a meditation on the creative and dynamic Word of God and the grace brought through the sacraments. One psychologist with whom I have talked who has pursued research on Pentecostalism for ten years declares that the group dynamics and the manipulation of the individual in the seminars are highly dangerous. Other psychologists, especially those who give therapy to ex-Pentecostals, are equally cautious. On a theological level these dynamics and manipulation might well hinder the deeper yet quieter working of the Spirit.

I suggest the following alterations:

(1) It would be advisable to have a reference to the Holy Eucharist or, at least, to one's denominational church in the commitment one is asked to make (*Team Manual*, pp. 10–11), for example, to attend the Eucharist whenever possible and to assist at Sunday service in one's denominational church.

(2) The Roman Catholic church by canon law forbids even a religious superior to insist on a manifestation of conscience; therefore one should not be obliged to share either one's religious experience or one's difficulties although one might promise to *attempt* to find a priest or recognized spiritual coun-

selor with whom one might commence a dialogue. The Pentecostal leaders should not intimate that they are the only ones capable of giving assistance.

(3) References to the kingdom of evil spirits behind the world's evil (p. 14) might be deemphasized.

(4) Similarly a person living a good Christian life should not be led to think of himself or herself as under the power of darkness (p. 16).

(5) The statement: "If you are unwilling to receive the gift of tongues, you are putting a block on the Lord's work and the Holy Spirit will not be free to work fully in you" should be revised.

(6) The *Manual* should show clearly that commitment is based on the renewal of baptismal vows in the Easter vigil. The prayer for tongues could include such a phrase as "if You wish" or "if it be Your will." Similarly, on page 28 the teaching on tongues could be moderated (see also p. 30).

Paraecclesial Structure

The *Team Manual* asserts: "Experience shows that if a person does not make connection with a group of other people living this new life, the Life in the Spirit Seminars will not make a major difference in his life." It is necessary to emphasize the importance of church life, for implicitly the *Manual* makes Pentecostal community appear more important than the church although it does state that God does not want us to leave the church (p. 160). However, the whole attitude of the leaders to their "authority" and "role" makes one fear that a complete paraecclesial structure, a Pentecostal magisterium exclusion, and an independent penitential system may arise. The team members see themselves as craftsmen "building the Church of God" (pp. 12–13). One would prefer the use of the word *re-*

store or the phrase "help to restore" and "part of the church" not "the church."

The Pentecostal leaders also see themselves as Spirit-inspired. In the words of the *Manual*: God "has entrusted his Spirit to them so that as they allow his Spirit to speak and act through them, others can meet him [God] in a new way" (pp. 22–23). Something could have been added about the Spirit-inspiration of the church herself and individual members who do not belong to the Pentecostal movement. After stating that they are Spirit-inspired, the Pentecostal leaders quote 1 Timothy 4:12, 16, a text that refers to Timothy, who was officially appointed to an office in the church, probably a bishopric. When speaking about the gifts that qualify the members for the team, the *Manual* says that a member must have the "kind of personal strength that inspires respect" (p. 25). One would have preferred the qualifications to be possession of the fruits of the Spirit, such as love, gentleness, and above all, humility. The leader takes the group and forms it into a community. He has the role of an elder in the Christian community (p. 28). It is asserted that "His life should be marked by the same characteristics that Paul recommended for overseers (supervisors, bishops, elders) in the Christian community (1 Tim. 3:1–7; Tit. 1:7–9)" (p. 28). Further, the chief leader is given the duty of teaching which is predicated of the bishop, but not of the man and woman deacons in the pastoral Epistles (see 1 Tim. 3:1–13). He gives many of the talks in the seminars, perhaps all, always the introductory talk, leads seminar 5, where people pray for the release, and gives the last section of the closing talk. Here there is risk of the development of a genuine paraecclesial structure and the dependence of the group on a hero-figure, especially since there is coaching in tongue speaking. Tight control with regard to the seminars is reflected in the statement, "Some small group of people should not decide on their own to offer the Life in the Spirit Seminars. Those who have the overall responsibility for the group should take responsibility for the seminars" (p. 65). This, of course, limits the free working of the Spirit.

Other small details are likely to trouble people. For example, participants in the seminar group are treated like children: an usher is appointed to direct them to their seats "and maintain order" (p. 82); they are given permission to leave after the registration, and so on. Further, the people coming to the seminars are "outsiders," distinct from the "insiders" within the group (p. 93). Finally, Clark states that God showed the Ann Arbor community how to develop the format of the seminars (p. 86). Whereas one must recognize that the Spirit is working in them, as he is in other Christians, the certainty with which the *Manual* asserts God's guidance and the fact that all the teaching of the seminar must be accepted (p. 24) makes one somewhat apprehensive.

Positive Approach: The Individual Sessions

Seminar 1: God's Love

Seminar 1, which has as its goal "to attract people to the seminar, to dispose them to turn to the Lord, to begin to stir up faith" (p. 89), is certainly constructive. It distinguishes among non-Christians, those who have fallen away from Christianity, and those living good Christian lives. It speaks of God's love and the importance of a personal contact with him. It would do better, however, to illustrate the fact that there is indeed authentic Christianity outside the Pentecostal movement. Although it mentions this, it does not pursue the matter far enough. Reference could be made to Cardinal Suenen's book A *New Pentecost?*

The *Manual* should also take into account the fact that the rules at Ann Arbor in the Word of God Community and in the People of Praise Community, South Bend, are much more rigid than in most religious congregations and that these strictures may well deter people from attending the seminars. Most importantly, however, in this seminar there should be an exposition of the modern teaching on the sacrament of baptism, especially for those who are Christians. As Protestant baptism is usually valid in the eyes of Catholics, it should present no difficulties. One could also compile Scripture readings about baptism and make a clear distinction between the sacrament and the release of the Spirit. If necessary, this could be printed in small type for the people who belong to sacramental churches, for example, Catholics, Episcopalians, and Lutherans. Such Scriptures as the baptism of Jesus (Matt. 3:13–17 and parallels) and the Lent cycle of Eucharistic readings such as the cure of Naaman and the cure at the pool of Bethsaida should be read. The object should be to show that baptism *does effect a real change.* For those who have already experienced baptism, baptismal vows could be renewed. Meditation on the liturgy for the adult baptism rite might well serve to rekindle the charism within.

The first seminar is also a good opportunity for scriptural instruction. As Karl Barth said, "The Word takes hold of you." By meditating on the Word the people will realize that it has a creative and dynamic power of its own, but particularly when it is heard at a Eucharistic gathering. To the advice on page 98 to pray every day to the Lord and meditate on his words could be added (in small print if necessary), "Try to attend the Eucharist each day, and note the stress on regeneration and covenant in the new canons of the Mass and listen to the appointed Scripture for the day."

Seminar 2: Salvation

The second seminar is designed to help people realize "that they are not just getting a 'blessing' when they are baptized in the Spirit, but they are committing themselves to a total re-orientation of life" (p. 101). This seminar might be better en-titled "Salvation and Sanctification." The current title of the seminar gives the impression that non-Pentecostal Christians are not saved. (Salvation should also be clearly distinguished from "eternal security.") For example, the seminar presents people with the opportunity to transfer from the kingdom of darkness to the kingdom of light (p. 101). One could say, however, that when God pours great light into the soul, we are made aware of the former darkness within our souls, not darkness caused by serious sin, but darkness relative to God's light. This seminar could provide an excellent occasion for modern teaching on the sacrament of penance, and in addition to non-Pentecostal Catholic books the candidates could be advised to read the Pentecostal books on penance, notably Father Francis Mac-Nutt's *Healing* and Father Michael Scanlon's *Penance*.

The seminar, however, concentrates too much upon what is wrong in the world and the hold of Satan over it (*Team Manual*, p. 105 f.). This might lead to Gnosticism or Manicheaen tendencies. Although it is true that there are problems and evils in the world, it is better to stress all the good that is in it, that Jesus has redeemed the world, that even creation groans for the adoption of the sons and daughters of God (see Rom. 8:22–23). Further, although it is, of course, correct that God can and will make new and wonderful changes in the world, this seminar does not mention mankind's responsibility to be a caretaker of the earth through a commission received from God (Gen. 1). With due deference to the *Manual* I should say that God wants man to use his wisdom and that the problems of the world should be solved by mankind using its wisdom in cooperation with God (p. 106). This seminar would be a good time to speak about various social action groups and to encourage people to work with these. The texts the *Manual* cites about Satanic influence in the world were used with reference to those who had *not accepted Christ* (pp. 106–7). Is it correct for the *Manual* to state "he [God] is now creating a new people, a new society in which men are free to live under God's rule and are free from the rule of Satan" (p. 108)? The kingdom of God began when Jesus walked this earth, not in the twentieth century.

Seminar 3: The New Life

This seminar focuses on the personal meaning for the individual of being baptized in the Spirit. One is happy to see that the *Manual* describes the seminar as one that will discuss a new life available through a "fuller reception of the Holy Spirit . . ." (p. 12). Therefore the talk can be directed to both non-Christians and Christians. However, one becomes a little nervous with the statement: "Full life in the Spirit begins when we are baptized in the Spirit" (p. 115), especially since the gift of tongues and the release of the Spirit are linked so closely together (pp. 155, 116).

The third seminar provides an excellent opportunity for teaching about the contemporary theology of the Eucharist where, indeed, Jesus gives us new life and nourishes that life within us. An exposition of the institution of the Last Supper in 1 Corinthians 11 and the Gospels and also a meditation and commentary on John 6 would be useful here. The emphasis on the Eucharist could replace the stress on tongues for those who belong to sacramental churches. In my experience, those who possess a deep faith in the Eucharist are less concerned with tongues. Alternately, or in addition, one could conduct a meditation on the new canons of the Eucharist, dwelling especially on new life and the role of the Spirit expressed in the canons.

Although much that Clark says in the *Manual* about baptism in the Spirit is good (in contrast to his book *Baptized in the Spirit*, pp. 51–52) and although he does state clearly that the Holy Spirit is given in baptism, it is perhaps better to view the release of the Spirit, not as a once-in-a-lifetime experience, but something that is repeated over and over again in different modalities throughout our Christian life. I believe that the release of the Spirit is a touch of infused contemplation and that one can dispose oneself to this but one cannot bring it about purely by human effort. It is well to make this quite clear. Passages of *The Graces of Interior Prayer* by Poulain would be worth studying, as well as the encyclical by Pope Leo XIII on the Holy Spirit.

Great caution should be taken with the scriptural passages the *Manual* uses to illustrate the baptism of the Spirit or, as the *Manual* prefers to call it, being baptized in the Spirit. Acts 2, Acts 8, Acts 10–11, and Acts 19 are cited (p. 125). Of these, Acts 2 is probably the best text to use. The disciples receive the fullness of Spirit, but there is no reference to the sacrament until the three thousand are baptized in the name of Jesus. Nor is it stated that the three thousand spoke in tongues. As I have said, Acts 8 is a difficult text. Nowhere else in the whole of the New Testament are people baptized without receiving the Holy Spirit; thus the Samaritan baptism is a unique event and should not be taken as normative. God obviously wished the Samaritans to have a very close union with the Jerusalem church and through his own special planning withheld the Spirit until Peter and John came from the Holy City. Thus the Samaritans would no longer be seen as a sect, inferior to the Jerusalem church.[2] Acts 10–11 (the Gentile Pentecost) and Acts 19 (the Ephesian Pentecost) are both sacramental baptismal texts. In Acts 10–11 the Gentiles receive the sacrament even though the Holy Spirit has fallen upon them, and in Acts 19 the dramatic gifts of the Spirit occur simultaneously with the sacrament of baptism. There is no doubt that Acts 19:1–7 is a sacramental baptism text *par excellence*.

One must also consider the possibility of reception of dramatic gifts *without* the release of the Spirit, that is, without an experimential sense of the presence of God. The dramatic gifts and the release cannot be said to be identical for, as Father Edward D. O'Connor has shown in his book *The Pentecostal Movement in the Catholic Church*, the release of the Spirit may be a purely inward experience (pp. 131–36; see also Tugwell, *Did You Receive the Spirit?*). O'Connor's explanation is to be preferred to Clark's and could with profit be quoted in full at this place in the *Manual*.

Seminar 4: Receiving God's Gift

The *Manual* calls the time of this seminar "how to do it" week, and places great emphasis on personal, human effort, both from the point of view of the candidate and that of the team members. It seems people cannot rely so much upon the free working of the Holy Spirit, but rather "concrete steps" must be taken "that will help them to be baptized in the Spirit" (p. 129). Incidentally, most of the seminars contain comments on the *dynamics*. In this seminar there is emphasis on repentance; therefore, it would be essential to have a priest present and to offer the candidates an opportunity for the reception of the sacrament of penance. The priest need not be Pentecostal. However, the *Manual* says nothing about the sacrament. It is possible, though, to place information concerning this in small type so that Catholics can use the advice conveniently and other Christians can pass it over if they wish.

In my experience many Protestants desire to receive the sacrament of penance, and arrangements could be made for it with their own ministers. It is very important that complete confidentiality be kept over the question of serious sin, but the Word of God Community does not seem to respect this confidentiality. The greeters must report to the team in writing, and then the information is transferred to the coordinators of the group. It could happen that eventually most of the community would know that such and such a person, for instance, has been on speed or heroin, lived in unlawful wedlock, and so on. At one time the Word of God Community maintained that it was important to announce people's sins to the whole community together with their names. Abundant counsel had to be given the coordinators before they realized that this was unwise. Public confessions and forced manifestation of conscience are reported in various groups. This does a great deal of harm.

The fourth seminar would be an ideal one in which to talk about the modern teaching concerning the sacrament of confirmation. The release of the Spirit is received (not acquired through personal effort) by disposing ourselves to a flowering of the gifts we received in baptism and confirmation. Further, if we have a religious profession, it would be an excellent idea to peruse the commitment service again and try to rededicate ourselves. Correspondingly, a priest or deacon (or other minister in non-Roman Catholic services) could meditate and relive his ordination service, perhaps even redramatize it. Women who are ordained ministers must not be asked to give up their ministry (this would be denying the grace and calling of God) but should be urged to recommit themselves. Roman Catholic women should be encouraged to seek God's guidance concerning ordination.

A most grace-filled action here would be a communal penance service with Catholics and people of other historical denominations receiving the sacrament individually and others joining in the rest of the service. There is no reason why non-Roman Catholic ministers should not assist in this service. The confessionals can be marked showing clearly to which denomination the minister belongs and also whether the minister is male or female. Women might like to receive the sacrament from female ministers, which would be possible in the Lutheran, Methodist, Presbyterian, and other denominations.

Seminar 5: Praying for Baptism in the Holy Spirit

The stated goal for Seminar 5 is "to help people make an authentic commitment to Christ, to help them to be baptized in the Spirit and speak in tongues" (p. 142). For Catholics I would think the best plan for this seminar would be to arrange for a celebration of the Eucharist and for the imposition of hands to take place at the offertory. In this way they can join in the totality of the Christian experience. The imposition of hands can be preceded by a renewal of baptismal promises and a rededication of oneself in view of the sacrament of confirmation. Imposition of hands can be performed by both Pentecostal and non-Pentecostal people. Perhaps a public Mass is the better choice since this means that the Catholic Pentecostals (or rather Pentecostal Catholics) join with the rest of the church rather than undergoing an individual, separate experience. Other denominations could hold their own services, and then all could come together for thanksgiving after communion, which could take the form of a prayer meeting with special emphasis on the candidates upon whom hands have been imposed using their new gifts. If possible a special feast day can be chosen for the day of imposition of hands.

Moreover, it is important to ask for the intercession and presence of Mary, for she was present at the first Pentecost and is considered as the "first Pentecostal" because of the descent of the Holy Spirit at the annunciation.

Further, instead of the exorcism that is performed (pp. 144, 145, 147–48), it would be better to pray for the presence of the angels—they will frighten away any evil spirit! The church is very hesitant to give permission for exorcisms and for significant reasons. Unofficial exorcisms can be harmful to the exorcist(s) and to the person over whom the prayers are recited. The fifth seminar overstresses the gift of tongues, and I would suggest that both the Rosary and the Jesus Prayer be explained at this session so that those who do not receive the gift of tongues may use an equally Spirit-inspired method of prayer. The recipient of the release of the Spirit can also be taught about the value of other forms of noncerebral prayer, especially the liturgy.

Seminar 6: Growth

The Sixth Seminar is "practical and instructional" and is meant to show people the way to grow in the life of the Spirit (p. 154). Here it is essential to emphasize, not so much Pentecostal community, but the community of the church and the difference between sects and religious congregations, the difference between being called to the religious life and being called to live an average Christian life without any special dedication. The candidates should realize that both are perfectly legitimate ways of Christian living; both are called by God and accepted and blessed by him. Pentecostal community or prayer group should be viewed as an optional way of life. Some of the most active Pentecostal Christians I know no longer attend prayer meetings. They do not deny the validity of their experience or the good of the movement, but they have found that the rules and regulations insisted upon by some Pentecostal leaders are too restrictive and quench the Spirit. Therefore, they have made their homes, their professional bodies, and their parish their Christian community, and they have launched forward and accomplished a great deal in church renewal. This would have been impossible if they had remained in the more restricted Pentecostal group.

Seminar 7: Transformation in Christ

The seventh seminar's goal is "to help people avoid discouragement over problems they experience, and to help them become a part of a charismatic community or prayer group" (p. 164). Here it would be good to list various societies or communities within the church to which people could belong. It is better not to present the Pentecostal group or community as the only viable option. It is also an advantage to invite non-Pentecostal Christians to speak to the group to explain various ways of living a life of the Spirit, for example, the cursillo movement, the Focolare movement, the Vincent De Paul, the thirty-day retreat movement, prayer house movement, and so on. It would be good, too, to supply the candidates with a book list which introduces or reintroduces them to traditional spirituality and to contemporary spirituality outside the Pentecostal movement and generally to make sure that the candidate does not think that the Pentecostal community is *the* Christian community or life rather than *a* Christian community or life. Pentecostalism has been called a spirituality by Rome, and this is the best way of approaching the movement. It is grace-bearing, but it is not for all. Even when one has received much through the seminars, one may feel that the Spirit leads on to further depth in prayer outside the Pentecostal community. Above all, the absolute necessity of belonging to the church and the importance of the sacraments must be emphasized. The continued use of the seminars as they are now organized could give rise to what, in effect, would be a new denomination.

Leadership and Community

In an attractive album containing four recordings on spiritual leadership (Cassette W 5001: Meyer, Talk 1; Brombach, Talk 2; Cavanar, Talk 3; and Ghezzi, Talk 4; with accompanying *Study Guide for Spiritual Leadership*) the national leaders of the Charismatic Renewal Services presented their teaching on spiritual leadership during 1972–74 in summary form. This was given to over six thousand leaders in the movement.

The first talk by Gabriel Meyer from Loyola University, Los

Angeles, is most encouraging. He offers four options: (1) the small prayer groups with the use of the Pentecostal gifts, which are informal and require no special commitment to the community; (2) the regional renewal meetings, which involve more leaders but have a varying attendance giving the group little stability; (3) a group of about forty or fifty people who attend a second meeting during the week that has some commitment from members, certain services, and the Life in the Spirit Seminars; (4) a formal community with an explicit commitment, several types of meetings, services, leaders, the Life in the Spirit Seminars, and Formation and Foundation Courses. Meyer maintains that it is important for groups to discern God's will and to seek the kind of community he desires. This might entail remaining small and informal. Discernment should also be applied concerning whether or not the group should be Catholic or ecumenical. Meyer emphasizes that there is no answer to this question. One may be obliged to live in tension or ambiguity, but it is imperative to live creatively. He also stresses the important balance between faith and common sense. His is a well-poised thesis and provides the maximum amount of freedom for members and for the Holy Spirit to work and move.

Jack Brombach, from a Minneapolis covenant group, gave the second talk. He refers repeatedly to God's plan for us and to the reason he has called us together. He advocates a community like those described in chapters 2 and 4 of Acts. He feels that the church does not allow room for community but that it is essential that we gather as the body and share things in common. He maintains that the Scriptures teach clearly that all people are not our brothers in the same way as those bound to us in the community. We must love other people, but there is a special love, akin to the marriage bond, with our Christian brothers and sisters. In the world, brotherhood is sought because of needs; it is a flesh-eating love, but the only love God can anoint is *agape*. In the Old Testament, Jews only considered fellow Jews as brothers. In the Christian church only truly committed Christians are our brothers. Brombach feels that he cannot even love his blood brother in a special way because he is not certain whether he is a Christian or not. Only in (covenant) agreement can God pour out his love. He recognizes the difficulty of belonging to two communities, as would happen in the case of a man or woman who belongs to a recognized Catholic religious congregation, but does not really find a solution to this. Although he warns against leaving the church or treating non-Pentecostal Christians as second-class citizens, the overall impression of the talk is that he feels the Pentecostal has to bring new life to the church—"God wishes to bring them into new life, too."

The third talk was given by James Cavnar from the Word of God, Ann Arbor. He speaks about wrong conceptions of leadership, that we cannot copy leadership patterns from the secular world and sometimes not even from the ecclesial world. He describes not only ambition and aggressiveness but also *democracy*. He avers that election by popular vote leads to factions and breaks down the relationship of the brothers. Another wrong approach, he states is the leaderless group (with only the Spirit leading); this produces deadness and problems. The alternative to these models is spiritual servanthood. Here leaders arise and have a certain permanency just as the organs of the body do. The mature members of the community choose other leaders.

The fourth talk was delivered by Bert Ghezzi, coordinator of the Word of God community and an editor of *New Covenant*. It summarized much of the information discussed in chapter 1.

The talks are completely devoid of Catholic content. There is no mention of the sacraments, the liturgy, church doctrine, or Catholic devotions such as veneration of Mary and saints or devotion to the Sacred Heart. No mention is made of the leadership or counsel of priests, bishops, or professional people.

Leadership is focused entirely upon lay Pentecostals, save for one brief note in the *Study Guide for Spiritual Leadership*: "priests should share authority with laymen." It is somewhat remarkable that the sentence does not read "Lay people should share authority with priests." Taken as a whole one must recognize that these four talks cannot be considered to be concerned with Catholic charismatic renewal. They are religiously indifferent.

Yet it must be admitted that this paternalistic, monarchical authoritarianism of Neo-Pentecostalism is making enormous strides, if success is to be measured by numbers.[3] However, some would question the durability of such a system, which appears to contrast so sharply with twentieth-century America. Are there not viable, contemporary options, which may not bring such "instant" results but which, as long-term policies, may serve the Neo-Pentecostal movement, society, and the church more effectively and, perhaps, more importantly, blend them together?

I would like to offer one suggestion from many that could be entertained, which borrows from the apparatus of sensitivity training.

First, it must be recognized that the fundamental difference between the Neo-Pentecostal group and the sensitivity group is that Neo-Pentecostalism has primarily a vertical dimension, that is, godwards (although it would appear that a human dimension has become more prominent recently), and the sensitivity group has mainly, but not exclusively, a horizontal dimension, that is, humanward. Second, however, it must be recognized that these are not mutually exclusive, precisely because they are not so in the incarnation. Both the Neo-Pentecostal group and the sensitivity group can learn much from each other.[4] Here I wish to talk about the ideal, professionally conducted sensitivity group, and I wish merely to note some insights (not, I believe, totally divorced from the wisdom of the Holy Spirit who dwelt in the incarnate Jesus and dwells now in his incarnate church) gained from the sensitivity group. These insights might be helpful to Neo-Pentecostals. I omit for the moment the advantages (of which I am sure there are many) on the other side.

The Nature of the Trainer

The nature of the trainer or facilitator in the sensitivity group contrasts sharply with the head in the house church or the community church within the Neo-Pentecostal group. The trainer is always a professional person, usually highly qualified, and may be either a man or a woman. Indeed, a man and a woman may work together in a complementary way as equals, recognizing that each sex has certain unique contributions to make. The trainer plays a nonteacher, nonmanipulative role, and his purpose is to "decrease" that the group may "increase" (see John 3:30). His or her behavior serves as a model to the rest of the group. For instance, if one of the members is experiencing a psychological crisis, the facilitator functions to create a supportive climate for the "sufferer," to work for healing and reconciliation together with the other members of the group. The trainer encourages a *collaborative concept of authority* by increasing the awareness of the *variety of leadership patterns* available.

Other Members of the Group

The group comprises those who are psychologically sound.[5] If members have had, or are having, therapy, their physician must give permission for their participation. They also work in a psychologically safe atmosphere. All the members of the group (men and women, old and young) are regarded as equal, and they are destined to undergo a learning experience from their peers within the group. The trainer expects to learn too. The structure of the group is minimal; indeed, the group finds what structure it wishes, and this is always open to change. There is a strong emphasis on inquiry, and the "feedback" system is intended to concentrate upon the "here and now" rather than the "there and then," unless a member wishes to volunteer certain information from the past. The feedback produces an alertness to human clues, that is, both verbal and nonverbal communication, and it is considered important that such communication be expressed in an atmosphere of trust and acceptance. This differs appreciably from the subordination concept in the Neo-Pentecostal group. Whereas the feedback is descriptive in the sensitivity group, in the Neo-Pentecostal group the very use of the texts concerning exclusion, which refer to immorality, greed, idolatry, reviling, drunkenness, theft, the cowardly, the unfaithful, the polluted, murderers, sorcerers, liars, the factious, and the perverted, is hardly calculated to build up a feeling of acceptance and mutual trust. Often the Pentecostal dialogue, if there is any, begins at a disadvantage. The disadvantage is on both the side of the accused and the side of the accusing. The "correction" can hardly be called descriptive, rather than evaluative, when these texts are used.

The Goals of the Sensitivity Group

Sensitivity groups engage in a new learning process—the production of an expanded consciousness, for example, aesthetic creativity, the role of fantasy and music, and the realization of latent potentialities within oneself and increase in self-esteem. They offer a wider recognition of available choices. For instance, with regard to behavior they offer a clarification of identity; a decrease in defensiveness; the unfreezing of expectations; the relinquishing of stereotypes and of submissiveness to authority patterns and the norms regulating intimacy. They engender an increase in sensitivity to others and aid in bridging the gap between self and others (which is very incarnational) and confirming one's fellow person.

The Results

Participation in a sensitivity group may produce a catharsis, which can be a very painful experience, involving negative emotional feelings. It is the role of the trainer to lead the group as a whole in assisting the individual through this painful experience to a constructive end. All are concerned for the member, and, instead of exclusion, the members go out of their way to persuade an "injured participant" to remain. After the sensitivity session there is often a follow-up by the concerned trainer.

This seems to be entirely different from the Pentecostal practice, judging from the evidence of the two Pentecostal communities I have observed. One group conducted a four-hour session of which there is a tape recording. When the session was arranged, the chairman announced that reconciliation was not the purpose of the meeting. During the session three persons delivered prepared written accusations lasting ten minutes each, and the accused was not permitted to speak, although time was allowed afterward. No word of kindness or encouragement or expression of positive feeling toward the accused was presented. The silence of the majority was eloquent. At the end of the four-hour session, only three out of the fifteen members present bade the accused goodnight, although the non-Pentecostals present revived the accused with a different kind of spirit! After the session no contact whatsoever was made with the accused even though he was a foreigner and lived alone. I do not mean to impute uncharity to the coordinators who conducted the session, for they really believed they were doing God's will. What I am saying is that the Pentecostal method of "accusing" and "shunning" thus appears entirely different from the concerns of the sensitivity group.

The sensitivity group increases a tolerance for living with ambiguity and for risk-taking behavior, as well as functional flexitivity; it reduces dogmatism. However the sensitivity group is a time-limited community which is destined to die; its members take away with them what they have learned in the group and are expected to apply it prudently and carefully to their personal lives. Thus it would seem that the sensitivity group offers food for thought for the Pentecostal, particularly in the realm of creative conflict.

On the whole, but not in every case, the Pentecostal reaction to conflict is "flight." This appears to be shown by the practice of exclusion, or giving those who hold different opinions a nonactive role in the community, or by a retreat into authoritarianism to quell individualism. These actions seem to suggest a feeling of deep insecurity among Pentecostal leaders. One might ask whether the fruits of the Spirit, such as humility, patience, love, and tolerance, so often found among the trainers and members of sensitivity groups, might assist the Pentecostal leaders to build up their self-esteem and open them to viable options that would allow more freedom of the Spirit within their communities. Did not the Master say that "the sons of this world are wiser in their own generation than the sons of light" (Luke 16:8)?

Abraham Maslow has constructed a chronological order of psychological development, which, simplified, is as follows: (1) physiological needs (hunger, thirst); (2) safety (security, order, stability); (3) love, belongingness (family affection); (4) identity (self-respect, self-esteem, success); (5) commitment (focus, direction); (6) self-actualization (creativeness, independence).[6] Type I Pentecostals appear to concentrate on level two. And perhaps this is appropriate to the stage of the life of their communities. Type II Pentecostals appear to range from levels three to six.

A Suggested Recipe for Pentecostal Delight

Pentecostalism has a great deal to offer the church, and I should like to conclude with a few suggestions for maintaining that which is good within it.

1. In *Varieties of Campus Ministry* Johnston states that the Word of God Community, Ann Arbor, "not only understands itself as called apart from the world; they see themselves as standing against Kierkegaard's 'vaporised Christianity, culture consciousness, the dregs of Christianity.' Like a good many younger Christians today, they judge that the greatest threat to the church's true life is not the secularism without but the pallid faith within" (p. 7).

In light of this statement, Pentecostal communities should realize the necessity of being as tolerant and supportive as possible. Exclusion is an instant sect creator. If, as a last resort, a participant must be asked to leave, he should continue to be prayed for and conversed with, in order to help him realize his spiritual potential. He certainly should not be ostracized. Leaders have two questions to ask—not only whether or not a given individual fits into the group but also, *do we of the Pentecostal community fit into twentieth-century American Catholicism?*

We cannot turn back the clock and relive the life of the early church as it is described in Acts 1–15. Even the Pauline churches in Asia Minor and the churches from which the Gospels of Matthew, Luke, and John emanated did not do that. They were flexible to the needs of the time and their particular localities. A sect is ahistoric and tries to recreate situations in the past irrespective of contemporary conditions. Churches accommodate themselves to everything good in contemporary culture. Thus, as Gabriel Meyer (Cassette W5001: Talk 1) demonstrates, we cannot have a master plan that serves the whole Pentecostal movement. Some Christians may find sufficient community in their family life, in their parish, or among their colleagues at work. It is important to understand this fully.

2. We must practice tolerance and forgiveness and never refuse the sacraments or the kiss of peace. We must accept people as they are, not as we would like them to be.

3. It would be advisable to avoid exorcism. It is significant that St. Paul does not list exorcism as one of the spiritual gifts (1 Cor. 12:10 does not necessarily refer to bad spirits, for in that case "unclean" would qualify "spirits" as in Acts 5:16). Further there are very few exorcisms in Acts and none in John. It is better to emphasize angels than demons, especially where children are concerned. We should encourage leaders to take training in a non-Pentecostal milieu. Training should include good Scripture exegesis, psychology, and sociology. There are many pastoral training centers for this throughout the country.

4. It would be beneficial for Pentecostal groups to rotate their leadership, employing both men and liberated women, priests and laity. In many religious orders, office is held only for three years or six at the most; this might be advisable for Pentecostal groups. Individuals could receive both the spiritual and the psychological screening which seminarians, deacons, and candidates for religious congregations are requested to undergo before acceptance into their vocation.

5. We must give the priest and bishop his appropriate place as leader and spiritual counselor and remember that he receives the fullness of the Isaiah gifts (see Isa. 11) at his ordination. The sacraments should be accorded central significance and communal penance services held for healing of dissension. It is not a good plan to have a separate Pentecostal Eucharistic

celebration that might take people away from the parochial or professional setting.

6. The divine office and other liturgical practices should complement the prayer meetings. In *The Holy Spirit and Power*, edited by McDonnell, Ranaghan has written an interesting essay on mainline Pentecostal services and their affinity with Catholic Pentecostal prayer meetings. He finds a parallel ritual activity. However, he should have drawn attention to the fact that two of the theological specialists in liturgical studies who were present at both Duquesne University and Notre Dame when the movement began have now withdrawn (p. 152). Further he states that people possessing special ministries and prophecies "are not distinguished or separated from the group as a whole" (p. 155). This contradicts Johnson (*Varieties of Campus Ministries*, p. 6) who describes the Ann Arbor open meeting. When he attended, the coordinators, all male, were in the center. The "next two rows on one side included those who would give prophecies for the evening"; they were male and female. Further "the witness had been routinised," and he found this rather contrived (p. 7). Moreover at the International Conference held at Notre Dame it was comical to see Pentecostal lay leaders on the platform, but the priests and bishops and the handicapped were tucked away with the *hoi polloi*, none of whom could use the microphone or exercise their ministries on any account. Liturgical practice, while controlling religious emotion, imagination, and enthusiasm, does allow everyone to participate.

7. For days of renewal, conferences, *and so on*, it is highly advisable to rotate speakers and to invite non-Pentecostal speakers, including psychologists and sociologists, so that a balance and a perspective is kept. One could also invite Pentecostal Catholics who are engaged in work outside the group but cannot or do not wish to attend the meetings regularly. Withdrawal from the group should not be called "defection." In an excellent book *The Charismatic Movement* Michael P. Hamil-

ton presented both sides of the movement, those who had had good experiences and those who had had disappointing ones. Books and conferences of this kind are almost imperative.

8. Many are becoming concerned about the increasing size of the movement. An increase in numbers always involves an increase in organization. Crowds are creative of structure, and I think most people would agree that there is enough structure within the church without creating more in the Pentecostal movement. Although I may be wrong, it seems to me that the Pentecostal movement or prayer meeting loses some of its *raison de'être* when it becomes organized. Let us keep meetings small. If necessary let us separate into smaller groups. We must consider carefully whether a "catechumenate" is advisable.

9. It might be a good idea for the prayer groups themselves to call a moratorium on prayer meetings for two or three months during each year. This would bring Catholic Pentecostals back into the mainstream of renewal within the church and make them realize their dependence upon the sacraments and the dispensability of the more dramatic gifts of the Spirit. Irvin (*Varieties of Campus Ministries*, p. 12) points out the need for more character diversity, "not massed produced sameness," and also for solitude. Precious little time is allowed for solitude in the community's regimen. Members find it hard to "go alone" before God and to seek him in their own interior voids and silences. They must be near geniuses when it comes to working and studying time since there's so little of it.

10. We must beware of shepherds and discipling. Type I Pentecostals use Juan Carlos Ortiz's book *Calling to Discipleship*. In an essay in the September–October 1975 issue of *Logos*, Charles Farah, Jr., states:

The story of Ananias and Sapphira, as far as the purity of the Church is concerned, is one of the most important miracles in the whole book of Acts. If Ananias and Sapphira had been allowed to lie to the Holy Spirit, if the early church had not purged those who broke the purity of its call and mission, the church could not have survived. And as difficult as Acts 5 is, it points out the power of God when the power of the Spirit runs high in the church. I suspect that as the church grows in power, we will see miracles like this occur again (p. 7).

Farah believes that denominationalism is a sin (p. 7), and he feels that extralocal authority could lead to an extralocal hierarchy. "Like Hamlet's father's ghost, there stands waiting in the wings the possiblity of a new charismatic denomination" (p. 8).

Farah finds that all the necessary elements are here—extralocal authority, apostles, financial structure, national conventions where speakers are meticulously screened. The next step is a "new full blown charismatic denomination" (p. 9).

11. Catholic Pentecostals should be careful not to segregate themselves from their non-Pentecostal friends and should be highly sensitive to the working of the Holy Spirit in every individual. Discernment largely consists in discerning *good, not evil* in people! They should be appreciative of the fact that their first obligation lies to their state in life, whether it is in the family or their profession. In *The Catholic Cult of the Paraclete* Fichter reports a charismatic from Massachusetts who fears that the movement may break from the church "unless we learn to avoid pride and a sense of separateness from our fellow Catholics" (pp. 59–60).

12. Social action and concern are essential. Fichter (pp. 87, 144) reports that the more heterodox were less likely to join in social change. He cites cases of people withdrawing into the haven of Pentecostalism because of frustration over social change. The washing of feet appears to be important to some of the national leaders, but it would be a pity if they thought they were fulfilling our Lord's precept merely by performing the ceremony. Far more powerful is the witness of the Loyola University, New Orleans, group who work to ameliorate conditions in underprivileged neighborhoods. They have fulfilled Jesus' precept.

13. Type I Pentecostals must develop a theology of the cross and of creative conflict. How much is the stress on healing and prayer for material advantages an evasion of responsibility and service?

Francis MacNutt's *Healing* is an excellent book; yet one would have liked to see in it a chapter devoted to nursing. How great is the charism and power of ordinary nursing—washing the patient, making his or her bed, doing countless acts of love which involve not only physical contact given with the gentleness and grace of the Spirit but also menial tasks which require revealing an ever-deepening sense of an appreciation of the dignity of the human being and a dramatic manifestation of the fruits of the Spirit. Type II has taken an interest in the theology of dying, but I know of no evidence that this is so in Type I.

14. There should be a thorough review of all Pentecostal books, pamphlets, and tape recordings sold by the Communications Center and at conferences as well as those circulating privately among the covenanted community. These should be reviewed by both Pentecostals and non-Pentecostals, and the object should not be to withdraw the material but merely to assess it. Books omitted from the catalogues of the Communications Center, such as Michael Hamilton's *The Charismatic Movement* and John Kildahl's *Psychology of Speaking in Tongues*, should also be reviewed.

15. The whole position of women needs much thought and prayer and, indeed, urgent attention. I have requested Kevin Ranaghan to permit me to prepare a tape recording that would complement the one produced by him and his wife, which teaches the submission of woman and the sole headship of men. As yet he has not replied. There is something frightening in the way women of Type I groups have become subordinate to the men. If the national leaders insist on a literal interpretation of Genesis and all the Pauline texts on women (they do not refer to Jesus' teaching), then, to be consistent, they must also work

for the restoration of slavery, which is accepted without question by St. Paul, and they must also embrace civil obedience, which is taught in Romans 13 but is not espoused by Jesus.

16. The regional (a word sharply criticized by the Advisory Committee) conferences could be released from the control of the national leaders and surrendered to the local bishop, his priests, sisters, and lay men and women in the various localities. Apparently this did happen in Atlantic City in 1975. The Holy Spirit would seem to have different plans for each diocese.

17. It would be highly beneficial to have a consultative body of Christians who are not all Pentecostals to deal with difficult problems. This could constitute a kind of "court of appeal."

18. Great diversity should be encouraged among the members of a Pentecostal group, a diversity of thought, a liberty of speech and talent. There should be a greater appreciation of the arts—which are a humanizing influence—and of the opportunities offered by the many non-Pentecostal movements for renewal within the church and, above all, an appreciation of the great intellectual gifts and opportunities now at our disposal. It is important, for example, to read non-Pentecostal literature as well as Pentecostal and to return to some of the great classics in Catholic literature. Literature should not be banned. In *Varieties of Campus Ministries* (p. 8) Johnson observes that the Ann Arbor group makes little reference to theology or biblical criticism. He adds, "One would wish for a little Augustine or Thomas Merton to balance the priority assigned to David Wilkerson's books." Further he avers that the Word of God Community is a distraction from the world of discursive scholarship.

It stands as an affront not only to churchly order; it violates the chief values of the academic world; it draws students out of preparation for "effective citizenship" and substitutes another world (p. 7).

Irvin asserts (p. 13) that God wants sons and daughters, not boys and girls.

19. We must study carefully all the fruits of the Spirit, especially love. The gifts may divide; the fruits always unite.

20. All of us must develop a sense of humor, particularly about our mistakes.

To recapitulate, Catholic Pentecostalism must go out into the main body of the church, not to convert or "evangelize" the converted, but to join hands with other Christians, to give and also to receive from them. This will make a mature body of Christ with perfect poise and proportion (see Eph. 4:11–16). As the structure of the church relaxes to allow greater freedom of vocation, Pentecostal men and women can grasp this opportunity and merge their leadership and other talents with that of the renewed church. I have seen nothing as pathetic as the sight of a baby with two heads. Such a child does not live long. On the spiritual level we may create such abnormality if "random Charismatics" rise to leadership separate from the rest of the church. Healthy Pentecostalism is integrated, and its life blood lies not only in preternatural gifts but also in the treasures of human and humane charismata.

NOTES

1. The qualifications required and quoted for a team leader are exactly those for a bishop (*Team Manual*, pp. 29–30). This points to a paraecclesial structure.

2. For further details see the excellent exegesis of these texts in F. F. Bruner's *The Theology of the Holy Spirit*.

3. I wish to thank Dr. Daniel Boland for his generous assistance in this section of the chapter. I have also consulted R. T. Golembiewski and A. Blumberg's *Sensitivity Training and the Laboratory Approach*; L. P. Bradford, J. E. Gibb, and K. D. Beene's *T-Group Theory and Laboratory Method*; and *Reading Book, Laboratory In Human Relations Training*.

4. One cannot deny, however, that in many Pentecostal groups there is a seeking for healing and reconciliation. An attempt to deal with conflict and problems is made by Stephen Clark on his cassette *Christian Personal Relationship*, but the method used is different from the sensitivity group. Clark advocates precise rules, agreements, or covenants even regarding such detailed behavior as the use of negative humor or indirect communication. He also prescribes a formula for asking for forgiveness and suggests that a penance should be given to the offender.

5. On his cassette *Dealing with Serious Psychological Problems*, Rauch estimates that one out of nine Pentecostals in the Ann Arbor community has serious psychological problems, but he states that one does not need a special charisma for dealing with these. In the Ann Arbor community these people are accepted into the full life of the group but are provided with a big sister or big brother; in another community they are excluded. I am not aware that Rauch has any psychological training. Unfortunately I was unable to hear the second part of the tape as the recording was too poor.

6. I am using a modified chart by Dr. John Kildahl, given to the Institute on the Charismatic Movement at Gunnison, Colorado.

Epilogue

I realize that this systematization of Catholic Neo-Pentecostal thought will cause anxiety or even anger to some and joy to others. I am loath to hurt anyone's feelings, but the national leaders of the Catholic Neo-Pentecostal movement have stated repeatedly that they are open to suggestions, questionings, and criticism. I hope they will respond to the book with courage and discernment. Already much of my thought has been incorporated in the circular on the Charismatic Renewal written by Father Richard Chachere of the archdiocese of Lafayette, Lousiana, and by Father Anthony Dilessi in an open letter to Dr. William Storey. I am confident that the leaders in Ann Arbor and South Bend will respond with equal generosity to the critique in this book and select anything which might promote the glory of God and the Father, God the Mother, and God the Son.

I place my work in the capable hands of Mary, the mother of Jesus, whose courage in the face of the dangerous charismatic ministry and teaching of her son has never been and never will be equaled.

Bibliography

A. BOOKS AND ARTICLES

Adams, J. E. *Christian Living in the Home.* Grand Rapids, 1975.

Beauvoir, Simone de. *The Coming of Age.* New York: G. P. Putnam's Sons, 1972.

Bender, Harold S. 2 vols. *Mennonite Encyclopedia.* Scottdale, Pa.: Herald Press, 1955.

Bittlinger, Arnold. "Baptized in Water and in Spirit." In *The Baptism of the Holy Spirit, as an Ecumenical Problem.* Edited by K. McDonnell and A. Bittlinger. Notre Dame, Ind.: Charismatic Renewal Services, 1972.

Bruner, F. E. *A Theology of the Holy Spirit.* Grand Rapids: Eerdmans, 1970.

Bradford, L. P.; Gibb, J. E.; and Benne, K. D. *T-Group Theory and Laboratory Method.* New York: Wiley, 1964.

Carothers, Merlin R. *Prison to Praise.* Plainfield, N.J.: Logos International, 1971.

Casey, Rick. Series of six articles in the *National Catholic Reporter.* "Whither Charismatics," 15 August 1975; "Charismatics II," 29 August 1975; "Charismatics III," 5 September 1975; "Charismatic Communities," 12 September 1975; "Charismatics V," 19 September 1975; "Charismatics VI," 29 September 1975.

Cavnar, James. *Prayer Meetings.* Pecos, N. Mex.: Dove Publications, 1969.

Chariton, Igomen, of Valamo. *The Art of Prayer.* Translated by E.

Kadloubovsky and E. M. Palmer. London: Faber and Faber, 1971.

Christenson, Larry. *The Christian Family*. Minneapolis: Bethany Fellowship, 1970.

──────. *A Charismatic Approach to Social Action*. Minneapolis: Bethany Press, 1974.

Clark, Stephen. *Baptized in the Spirit*. Pecos, N. Mex.: Dove Publications, 1970.

──────, ed. *The Life in the Spirit Seminars Team Manual*. Notre Dame, Ind.: Charismatic Renewal Services, 1973.

Cohn, Norman. *The Pursuit of the Millennium*. New York: Harper & Row, 1961.

Danielson, D. "A Community of Pentecostals." *Sisters Today*, December 1971, pp. 215–24.

DeCelles, Paul. "Reflections on the 1973 Conference." *New Covenant*, July 1973, pp. 24–25.

de Zutter, Patricia McCarty. "Authority 'Rests on Male Shoulders.' " *National Catholic Reporter*, October 1975, p. 6.

Fichter, Joseph. "How It Looks to a Social Scientist." *New Catholic World*, November/December 1974, pp. 246–47.

──────. *The Catholic Cult of the Paraclete*. New York: Sheed and Ward, 1975.

Ford, J. Massyngberde, and Keifer, Ralph. *We are Easter People: A Commentary on the Lectionary Readings for Lent and Easter*. New York: Herder and Herder, 1970.

Ford, J. Massyngberde. *The Spirit and the Human Person*. Cincinnati: Pflaum Press, 1969.

──────. *The Pentecostal Experience*. Paramus, N.J.: Paulist Press, 1970.

──────. *Baptism of the Spirit*. Chicago: Claretian Fathers, 1971.

──────. *Six Pentecosts*. Pecos, N. Nex.: Benedictine Monastery, 1976.

──────. "Pentecostal Catholicism." *Concilium*, vol. 9, no. 8 (1972), pp. 85–90.

──────. "Roman Catholic Communion." *Dialog*, vol. 13 (Winter 1974), pp. 45–50.

──────. *The Hospital Prayer Book*. Paramus, N.J.: Paulist Press, 1975.

──────. *The Way of Resurrection*. Notre Dame, Ind.: Fides Press, forthcoming.

————. "Pentecostal Poise or Docetic Charismatics." *Spiritual Life*, vol. 19, no. 1 (1973), pp. 32–47.

————. "A Note on Proto-Montanism in the Pastoral Epistles." *New Testament Studies*, vol. 17, no. 3 (1971), pp. 338–46.

————. *Ministries and Fruits of the Spirit*. Notre Dame, Ind.: Catholic Action Press, 1972.

————. "Biblical Material Relevant to the Ordination of Women," *J. of Ecumenical Studies*, vol. 10, no. 4 (1973), pp. 669–94.

Garrigou-Lagrange, R. *The Three States of the Interior Life*. London: B. Herder, 1951.

Gelpi, Donald L. *Catholic Pentecostalism*. Paramus, N.J.: Paulist Press, 1971.

————. *Pentecostal Piety*. Paramus, N.J.: Paulist Press, 1972.

Geraets, David. *Baptism of Suffering*. Pecos, N. Mex.: Benedictine Monastery, 1970.

————. *Jesus Beads*. Pecos, N. Mex.: Dove Publications.

Golembiewski, R. T., and Blumberg, A. *Sensitivity Training and the Laboratory Approach*. Itasca, Ill.: Peacock Publications, 1970.

Hamilton, Michael P. *The Charismatic Movement*. Grand Rapids: Eerdmans, 1975.

Hembree, C. R. *The Fruits of the Spirit*. Grand Rapids: Baker Book House, 1969.

Herschberger, G. P., ed. *The Recovery of the Anabaptist Vision*. Scottdale, Pa.: Herald Press, 1962.

Hilton, Walter, *The Ladder of Perfection*. Translated by L. Sherley-Price. London: Penguin, 1957.

Hokoema, A. *Baptized in the Spirit*. Grand Rapids: Eerdmans, 1972.

Hyde, Douglas. *Dedication and Leadership*. Notre Dame, Ind.: University of Notre Dame, 1970.

Hollenweger, Walter. *Pentecostals: The Charismatic Movement in the Churches*. Translated by R. A. Wilson. Minneapolis: Augsburg, 1972.

James, William. *The Varieties of Religious Experience*. New York: New American Library, 1958.

Johnson, Robert. "The Word of God Community at Ann Arbor." In *Varieties of Campus Ministries: Seven Studies*. Cambridge, Mass.: Church Society for College Work, 1973.

Jones, James W. *Filled with New Wine*. New York: Harper & Row, 1974.

Julian of Norwich. *Revelation of Divine Love*. Translated by James Walsh. New York: Harper & Row, 1961.

Kadloubovsky, E., and Palmer, G. E. H. *Writings from the Philokalia on Prayer of the Heart*. London: Faber & Faber, 1967.

Kelsey, Morton T. *The Art of Christian Love*. Pecos, N. Mex.: Pecos Benedictine Press.

Kildahl, John. *The Psychology of Speaking in Tongues*. New York: Harper & Row, 1972.

Life in the Spirit Seminars Team Manual. Notre Dame, Ind.: Charismatic Renewal Services, 1973.

Littell, Franklin H. *The Anabaptist View of the Church*. Boston: Star King Press, 1958.

———. *The Origins of Sectarian Protestantism*. New York: Macmillan, 1952.

———. *The Free Church*. Boston: Star King Press, 1957.

———., ed., *Reformation Studies*. Richmond, Va.: John Knox Press, 1962.

MacNutt, Francis S. *Healing*. Notre Dame, Ind.: Ave Maria Press, 1974.

Malone, Terry. "Ignatius House: An Experience in Pentecostal Community." *New Catholic World*, November/December 1974, pp. 266–70.

Martin, Ralph. "How Shall We Relate to Church?" *New Catholic World*, November/December 1974, pp. 251–52.

———. *Unless the Lord Build the House*. Notre Dame, Ind.: Charismatic Renewal Services, 1971.

McCann, Justin, ed. *The Cloud of Unknowing and Other Treatises*. Westminster, Md.: Newman Press, 1952.

McDonnell, K., ed. *The Holy Spirit and Power, the Catholic Charismatic Renewal*. New York: Doubleday, 1975.

Mumford, Bob. *Living Happily Ever After*. Old Tappan, N.J.: Fleming H. Revell, 1973.

New York Times. "Charismatic Movement Facing Internal Discord Over a Teaching Called 'Discipling!' " 16 September 1975, p. 31.

Nouwen, Henri J. *Intimacy*. Notre Dame, Ind.: Fides Press, 1970.

———. *The Wounded Healer*. New York: Doubleday, 1972.

O'Connor, Edward D. *The Pentecostal Movement in the Catholic Church*. Notre Dame, Ind.: Ave Maria Press, 1971.

———. "When the Cloud of Glory Dissipates." *New Catholic World*, November/December 1974, pp. 271–75.

Peers, Allison E. *Studies in the Spanish Mystics*. 3 vols. 2d ed. London and New York: Macmillan, 1951.

Philips, Dietrich. "Twelve Notes on the Church." In *Spiritual and Anabaptist Writers*. Library of Christian Classics, edited by George Williams, vol. 25. Philadelphia: Westminster Press, 1957.

Poulain, A. *The Graces of Interior Prayer*. London: Routledge & Kegan Paul, 1957.

Pourrat, P. *Christian Spirituality*. Vols. 1–3: London: Burne Oates, 1924. Vol. 4: London: Newman Press, 1953.

Pulkingham, W. Graham. *Gathered for Power*. New York: Morehouse-Barlow, 1972.

Ranaghan, Dorothy, and Ranaghan, Kevin. *As the Spirit Leads Us*. Paramus, N.J.: Paulist Press, 1971.

Randall, John. *In God's Providence, The Birth of a Catholic Charismatic Parish*. Locust Valley, N.Y.: Living Flame Press, 1973.

Robison, James. "Charismatic Movement Faces Growing Rift." *Chicago Tribune*, 11 October 1975, p. 11.

Ross, Elisabeth Kübler. *On Death and Dying*. New York: Macmillan, 1972.

Scanlon, Michael. *The Power of Penance*. Notre Dame, Ind: Ave Maria Press, 1972.

Schaupp, Joan. *Women, Image of the Holy Spirit*. Denville, N.J.: Dimension Books, 1975.

Sherrill, John L. *They Speak with Other Tongues*. New York: McGraw Hill, 1964.

Storey, W. G. "Charismatics—Serious Problems." *A.D. Correspondence*, vol. 10, no. 11 (1975).

———. *Morning Praise and Evensong*. Notre Dame, Ind.: Fides Press, 1973.

———. *Praise Him*. Notre Dame, Ind.: Ave Maria Press, 1973.

———. *Bless the Lord*. Notre Dame, Ind.: Ave Maria Press, 1974.

Suenens, L. J. Cardinal. *A New Pentecost?* Translated by Francis Martin. New York: Seabury Press, 1975.

Tugwell, Simon. *Did You Receive the Spirit?* Paramus, N.J.: Paulist Press, 1973.

Underhill, Evelyn. *The Mystics of the Church*. New York: Schocken, 1971.

Wenger, J. E., ed. *The Complete Works of Menno Simons*. Scottdale, Pa.: Herald Press, 1956.

Williams, George. *The Radical Reformation*. Philadelphia: Westminister Press, 1962.

Williams, George, ed. *Spiritual and Anabaptist Writers*. Library of Christian Classics. vol. 25. Philadelphia: Westminster Press, 1957.

Wueller, F. S. *Release for Trapped Christians*. Nashville, Tenn.: Abingdon, 1974.

Yoder, John H. "Binding and Loosing." *Concern*, February 1967.

Zablocki, Benjamin. *The Joyful Community*. Baltimore: Penguin, 1971.

B. CASSETTES

Unless otherwise noted, the following cassettes are released by the Communications Center, Notre Dame, Indiana.

Brombach, Jack. *Building Christian Brotherhood*. Cassette W 5001. Talk 2.

Cavnar, James. *What Is Spiritual Leadership?* Cassette W 5001. Talk 3.

Clark, Stephen. *Serving as Head in Christian Community*. Cassette 1127.

————. *The Elder in Christian Community*. Cassette 1126.

————. *Growth of the Community Service Group*. Cassette 112.

————. *The World and Christian Community*. Cassette 1103.

————. *Christian Personal Relationships*. Cassette 120.

Cohen, Harold. *Priest and the Charismatic Renewal: The Priest's Full Life in the Spirit*. Cassette 120.

DeCelles, Paul. *Christian Living Situations*. Cassette 121.

Geraets, David. *Christian Community, Shared Prayer, Shared Living*. Cassette 137.

Ghezzi, Bert. *Spiritual Growth for Leaders*. Cassette W 5001. Talk 4.

Koller, Kerry. *Christian Community*. Cassette 122.

Maloney, George. *The Jesus Prayer*. John XXIII Centre, Electronic Paperbacks, Fordham University, The Bronx, New York 10458.

Meyer, Gabriel. *Essential Elements for Building Prayer Groups*. Cassette W 5001. Talk 1.

Martin, Ralph. *Pastoral Situations Which Aid Initiation.* Cassette
    110.
————. *Christian Initiation.* Cassette 109.
————. Cassette 116.
Quinn, John. *The Spirit in the Sacraments.* Cassette 152.
Ranaghan, Kevin. *Survey of the Catholic Charismatic Renewal.*
    Cassette 125.
Randall, John. *Growth and Decline of Prayer Groups.* Cassette 156.
Rauch, Gerry. *Dealing with Serious Psychological Problems.* Cas-
    sette 157.
Scanlon, Michael. *Penance.* Cassette 158.
Songy, B. *Religious Communities and the Charismatic Renewal.*
    Cassette 127.

C. OTHER SOURCES

Directory: Catholic Charismatic Prayer Groups, June 1974. Pub-
    lished by Charismatic Renewal Services, Notre Dame, Ind.
Pecos Benedictine Newsletter. Issued by the Benedictine Monastery,
    Pecos, N. Mex.
Ranaghan, Kevin. *Statement on Behalf of the Catholic Charismatic
    Renewal Service Committee,* May 30, 1975. Communications
    Center, Notre Dame, Ind.
Reading Book. rev. ed. Laboratory In Human Relations Training,
    Institute for Applied Behavioral Science, 1969.
Report of the Word of God Community. Word of God Com-
    munity, Ann Arbor, Mich., 1971.
Second Statement of the U.S. Bishops. In *Origins,* 2 June 1972,
    pp. 60–61.
Southern California Renewal Community Newsletter. Issued by the
    Southern California Renewal Community, Los Angeles, Calif.
*Statement from the Notre Dame–South Bend Service Board Con-
    cerning N.* Mimeographed.
True House Covenant Commentary. Mimeographed.